I and God are One

Loving Light Books

Also by Liane Rich:

Loving Light

Book 16

I and God are One

Liane Rich

The information contained in this book is not intended as a substitute for professional medical advice. Neither the publisher nor the author is engaged in rendering professional advice to the reader. The remedies and suggestions in this book should not be taken, or construed, as standard medical diagnosis, prescription or treatment. For any medical issue or illness consult a qualified physician.

ISBN 13: 978-1-878480-16-3
ISBN 10: 1-878480-16-2

Loving Light Books:
www.lovinglightbooks.com

Also Available at:
Amazon - www.amazon.com
Barnes & Noble - www.barnesandnoble.com

for Ana Maria

The information in this series is not necessarily meant to be taken literally. It is meant to *shift* your consciousness...

Foreword

Anyone immersed in the vast body of new metaphysical knowledge is aware of the virtual symphony of voices from channeled sources throughout the world - inspirational voices that may be artistic, poetic, philosophical, religious, or scientific. And now, out of these myriad New Age voices, comes a series of books by God, channeled through Liane, revealing the frank truth in all its glory and wonder, telling us how to cleanse our bodies, gain access to our subconscious minds, clear our other selves and march back to who we are - God.

In God's books you will be introduced to a loving, powerful, gripping, exciting, and often humorous voice that reaches out and speaks ever so personally to the individual reader. As the reader's interest deepens, invariably an intimate relationship to this voice develops. It is a relationship that lasts forever, and I am quite certain I do mean forever.

Here is an accelerated program, a no-holds-barred course, where God guides us and loves us, and as needs be recommends books to us and even a movie or musical piece along the way. He (She) enters our lives and sees through our eyes, seeming to enjoy the ride as He guides us back to US, back to ALL. Here is a voice that is playful and informative, that is humorous and serious, that is gentle and powerfully divine. It is a voice that knows no barriers or restrictions, a straightforward and honest voice that caresses us when we need the warmth and pushes us when we are immobilized.

In today's New Age literature there is an avalanche of information from magnificent beings of light, information that possesses us and compels us to look at our fears and express our love. In this series of books by God, you will find truly powerful methods for making this transition from toxicity to purity, from density to light, from fear to love, and from the delusion of death to the awakening to full life. You will experience in these books the love and the power of God for it is your love to express and your power to behold. Rarely will you see more lucid steps for transformation. Read these beautiful words and rejoice in our period of awakening, our return to Home.

John Farrell, PhD., LCSW. - Psychologist, Clinical Social Worker, Senior Clinician Psychiatric Emergency Services, U.C. Davis Medical Center, Sacramento. John is also a retired Professor - California State University, Sacramento, in Health Sciences and Psychology.

I and God are One

Introduction

 As you begin to take your first steps towards enlightenment, you will go through many different phases. You will begin to feel as though you are no longer in control of your life and you will begin to feel as though you are being pushed and shoved through your own debris and subconscious programming. Once you begin to take on light, or enlightenment, you begin to turn you around and put you outside of your own programming. You begin to lose control by losing the rules you always played your games or patterns by. You begin to receive new information and, gradually, this new information will become you. It takes time! All healing takes time. It is not necessary to believe that you are trapped in time, but since you work and live and play in this time dimension you will find that time is here to assist you, as all things are here to assist you.

You are beginning a process that will give way to new insight and significant new intelligence. This process is the process of *becoming*. It is the process of becoming God and it has little to do with becoming ego. You all want what you can't have because you have been programmed to "strive for more." When you let go of this type of mentality you will begin to realize how much you have, and appreciate how much you have. Sometimes less (in the material world) is actually a gift. The less material the more you may receive. If you are full of material needs you may never require anything and therefore never require God's assistance in your life. If you do not ask, God does not enter. If you ask you shall be received and in being received you shall be redeemed.

Redemption is a very big step for you. You are allowed to take your own self and realize that you and God are hand-in-hand. You are allowed, at redemption, to return what you know in order to receive what you are not willing to know. Redemption will free you from your programmed beliefs and ideas that have caused you fear. Redemption is a way of changing you and allowing you to be all that you can be. Redemption is a way of facing what you fear in order that you might no longer fear it. If you face it and see it for what it is you will no longer fear it. Fear is the illusion that creates the pain that blocks out the joy. You will learn through this process of redemption that, not only do you fear God, you also fear being God. This is a very big step for you to take. You have always put God outside of yourself and you have always put God on an impossible pedestal. God is not what you believe. God is you and you are one with God.

This is what you will discover as you read the pages of this book. As you know, these books have been channeled in a manner that will gradually lead the reader into his or her subconscious self and explore the possibilities or programming, which leads to retraining the thought process, which allows for broader thinking (expansion), which will ultimately expand the awareness and make room for more of you (God) to enter you.

When we first begin to take on light we will find that it is a process of opening up to new possibilities and of being free of old set values. You begin to open by letting yourself expand and you begin to expand by being free of restriction. Restriction is caused by limitation and limitation is any fear or judgment that you may hold.

As you begin to open to the light you will begin to change your fears and your judgments into something less limiting and binding. You will begin to see how you are no longer in need of such limitations and you will begin to see how much harm they can be. When you open to the light you allow your fear to come to the surface and to be faced and dealt with. Many of you will experience emotional pain as you release your fears. At the least you will experience mild headaches and at the most you will experience great fear (stress, anxiety, emotional upset and physical upset). You will experience whatever is *in* you already, as it is now coming up and out of you. Do not despair. You are not losing you, you are losing fear. It is the part of you that is holding you back, and creating pain in your life, that is going. You are becoming God. Fear is becoming less as you become light. You are leaving all the garbage behind in order to rise up. You are becoming a "light" being and you are learning how fear feels so that you may consciously choose love over fear at any given moment.

When you have times of great sorrow and stress, remember that you are simply learning who you are and how you feel. You may change any feeling by knowing it and releasing it. You may learn to know you by allowing you to feel and to express what you feel. There is a great deal of confusion about expression. You do not need to get on a soapbox and express your feelings and you do not need to be in a group to express your feelings. You may express to you. You have never been taught to speak with you. You are taught to confide in others and to assume that they can give good advice. Speak directly to you. You are not crazy to talk to you. You lock people up for talking to themselves and this is due to ignorance.

You will find that communication, as good therapy, begins at home. You are not nuts if you speak to you. Love you enough to speak to you. You have always ignored you. You look to others to speak to you and to comfort you and even to hold you. Why do you not hold you and comfort you and speak softly and sweetly to you? Do you not love you? Do you expect others to do it for you? Yes. You are taught to search for comfort and nurturing outside of yourself and I will teach you to love and to nurture you. The object of these books is to bring love into you. You are not here to be left alone and unloved. You are here to learn love, pure and simple. No one ever taught you to love yourself. You were taught, however, to search for love outside of you.

You are going to find that not only do you not know how to communicate with yourself; you also do not know how to be you. You are so confused about who you are that you often adopt the behavior and attitude of another just to please and to be accepted by them. This is seen very often in childhood and is also prevalent in adult behavior. It is especially seen in courtship and in male/female or romantic relationships. I believe you call it a honeymoon. A spouse or lover acts and behaves one way until the romance is solidified and then the real self begins to act out and be seen. This is a form of giving yourself away in order to receive attention, love and nurturing. What you are going to learn as we continue our books is that once you love you it will be acceptable for you to be you. You will not feel the need to give you away in order to "receive." You will begin to see how you are well worth keeping and knowing and loving and you will begin to love you and know you and you will wish to keep you.

This is how you will begin to be God. God is you and you and God are one. Do not give up on God (you). Do not give up on love (you). You will be feeling many things that do not feel like love and these are the distortions of your past. Allow the distortions to come up and out of you and you will become clear and bright. You are learning to shine and you must be free of the darkness you have created. All darkness is actually distorted light. All light comes from God. There is only God, and the source that is God is now taking over and clearing things up.

❧

*W*hen you begin to know yourself you will be learning how to overcome everything that makes up your current belief system. You will be learning to see how you are no longer part of what you believe and you will become what you have always been under all that programming. It is not necessary for you to learn everything about you, for you are so vast that you are very widespread. If you begin to know the basics of what you have become due to programmed influences, you will be able to unravel the web enough to give you some freedom. A little freedom will make you feel very good. You have been darkness for so long that you cannot see the light when it is shown to you.

You will find that as you begin to see things from a new perspective you will begin to realize how you no longer wish to be in the dark. Many of you have false beliefs and have structured an entire reality out of these lies. When you are ready to let go of the lie you will be ready to move ahead into truth. "The truth hurts" is a saying that can be changed. It does not necessarily hurt. You have made certain situations painful for yourself by allowing yourself to believe that you will get hurt in some way. Usually this is connected to an emotional hurt, or getting one's feelings hurt to the extent that one can no longer put their feelings on the line. You will learn that feelings do not hurt you. You need feelings to know how you are, at any given moment. You are in charge of your feelings and you need not depend on others to take care and safeguard your feelings. You take care of your feelings, and trust you to know you enough to not allow you to take on more than you are ready for.

When you begin to deal with your feelings you will be dealing with the biggest part of you. Feelings have gotten you where you are today and feelings are your sensory output and input. They allow you to know yourself and they allow you to sense what is going on around you. Your feelings can be powerful but they can also mislead you if you have been dealt with unfairly in your past. When you project old feelings into a new relationship or situation you are repeating patterns and cycles. Sometimes you draw people to you who will re-create the exact feeling situation that caused an original pain. This will then allow you to see this pain for what it is and to let go of any judgment you may carry against the situation.

You are learning at this time to move out of pain and to allow yourself to be your own guide and your own caretaker. It is not necessary to give your feelings over to another and expect them to take good care of your feelings and sensitivities. You are in charge of you. You live in you and you will eventually learn to be responsible for how you think and how you feel. You are going to transform and to change how you care for your "self." Self is the part of you that is inside under all that garbage you believe to be necessary for survival. The garbage is coming off and up and out of you and you will be left with only "self." When you become "self" you become all that you are. The self is the part of you that is growing not dying. The "self" is the part of you who is God. The "self" is you. The rest is a lie that is being peeled away so that you might expose your "self" to the world.

When you begin to see how your feelings have led you astray you will begin to know that you are no longer in charge of you. You have been trained to reflex or respond in a certain way. Now you are being retrained and you are learning that there are an unlimited number of ways to handle any given situation. Once you learn this you will give up positionality because you will no longer be able to stand in one position solidly. You will move into the flow and out of judgment. This may "feel" like wishy-washy to you because you are taught (very strongly taught) to take a position and fight for your rights and stand up for what you believe. This attitude gets you stuck and un-flexible. Now you are learning that anything is possible and there is no one way, nor one position. There are as many ways and positions as there are possibilities. And since you already know that absolutely anything is possible, you are open to absolutely anything... this includes feelings.

There is no set way to feel. You may experience no feeling or all feelings in any given situation. Most of you do not recognize a feeling when you are having one. You simply take a pill, or drink some coffee to re-stimulate and charge yourself so you will not have to feel "you" (self). You are so accustomed to that coffee break and cigarette break that you do not realize how you are shutting "you" (self) off every time you take a sip or a puff. I don't tell you to stop drinking caffeine and smoking nicotine because I am a health fanatic. I tell you because you are wanting to wake up and yet you are shutting your "self" down at the same time. You are creating chaos and struggle for your own "self." When you learn to release and free the "self" you will no longer feel so much pain. Once you free the self you will move into higher thinking and higher feeling vibrations. This will allow you to be much more expansive in your feelings. It will bring you up out of the base feelings of fear and stress and pain. You will move into higher realms of love and joy and peace.

Now; when you begin to open your feelings and let them out, you may find a flood of emotions that are built up and highly charged. Do not freak out and think that you are losing it! Well, actually you are losing it, as you are losing these stored up feelings of hostility that are so highly charged. When you allow these feelings to surface do not be afraid of them. Move gradually through them and allow them to discharge and disperse. You will be allowed to feel whatever is in you and to some of you this will be very upsetting, but please do not blame others for your upset. It is all you clearing you; and others are assisting by pushing just the right buttons in you to get you to "go off." If you "go off" you discharge and release what explosives you are carrying. It's like I told you in the past, you are ticking time bombs and it is time to discharge and dismantle your explosive side.

Before you begin to heal, you will begin to feel your illness. Many of you do not know that you are sick and deprived. You believe you have always been okay the way that you are and you do not realize that you have a wound in you. You believe that life is just not that joyous all the time and that it is to be expected. This is your illness. You are to expect joy at all times and to live in bliss. If you had no wounds you would not have to teach each new generation how to "fight" for their rights and how to "cope" with life. To come into a world where you are immediately taught to "fight" and to "cope" is enough to bring anyone down a little. What if you had no wounds from past existences and you could not turn everything into drama and pain? You might actually enjoy the simple act of living. You would not require certain gifts to make you feel fulfilled. You would only require breathing in and breathing out.

As you learn to heal your wounds you will be restoring joy to your life. This healing process may take some time depending on how severely wounded you have been. You will learn that not only do you require time to heal; you also require time to learn. You must learn how to love you. This is new to you and was not taught by your parents. How could they teach you what they do not know?

So; how do we go about this job of healing the wounds so that we might love the self? We first must look at the wound and see how infected it is or how much charge is around it. Next we must drain the infection and allow the wound to discharge all the extra energy that is built up in it. After the wound has drained and discharged some of its power over you, you will be allowed to see what the wound was caused by. This could be a multi-level wound that has a great deal of cause and effect or it may be a big wound in only one area, depending on how you received it and processed what you received. Once you have looked at the now drained and discharged wound you may begin to apply salve. This salve could be understanding or kindness or caring. It does not matter where you start as long as you put something healing where you were drained. It could be that you simply need to slow down your life and remain calm. This is often a good ointment for freshly discovered wounds. You will want to take care of you and to nurture yourself.

Often, when you first discover a wound, you do so by examining your life and seeing what is not joyful or what seems painful. This is not the only way, however, to discover wounds. You may begin to walk into a situation and find it very painful. This is a signal that something is hurting you that should be looked at. All too often you believe it is the situation when, in actuality, it is you being pushed into a part of you that you do not wish to look at. As you begin to discover these parts of you that you do not wish to look at, I want you to remember to not judge. Do not judge you and do not judge your situation. You are giving yourself a big gift by giving yourself a situation that will show you how you are wounded.

As you begin to grow stronger and to heal, you will be able to walk into situations without falling down or falling apart, or "without fear." When you can enter situations without fear you will be living your life "without fear." You will be open to joy in every situation. You will be looking for the bliss and the good in all life experience. You will no longer see your world as a fear-filled world; you will see it as a love-filled world. You will also begin to see you as love-filled and no longer fear-filled. You will have drained you of all that excess energy in your wound. That energy is built up fear energy and it stops you from enjoying life and people and situations that cause you to expand.

Your expansion is blocked by your fear of exploring and growing because you were hurt in certain areas of your psyche when you were born. You came into a world that did not know how to teach you to love you and this is how you lost self-love and self-esteem. You are not prepared to love yourself and therefore you cannot love your life. When you drain the wound and retrain the psyche, you will be allowed to see all life from a whole new perspective and you will be allowed to see you from a whole new perspective. You will no longer put you down and you will no longer judge you. You will know when you have gotten to this state, as you will be joyful and you will no longer feel that life is a struggle.

*W*hen you begin to feel your own pain you will begin to release your hold on it. Many of you do not know that you are in pain and you walk around thinking this is just how you are. You even think you are above others who are in pain and confusion. If you constantly see other people's problems and not your own you are probably the one with problems. You are seeing their problems in order to direct your focus away from your own pain which is too great for you to look at. This is very common with parents who try to fix their children, and spouses who try to fix their mates. You will find that, more often than not, you are looking at a direct reflection of yourself. If you do not have children or a mate you will see your patterns in coworkers or any other family type situation you might be in. As in all relationships, you are learning about you and this is why you are in the relationship to begin with. You will see you in anyone you look upon because you cannot see what you do not carry. If it is part of you, you project it out so that it comes back to you from outside of you but it really starts *in* you.

You have begun to heal a great deal of confusion by becoming aware of this fact. As you heal confusion you must let go of the pain that was created by the confusion. When you learn that you are being programmed in order to heal old ways of thinking and acting, you will be grateful for all that you are seeing at this time. You are looking at you and this takes a great deal of trust in yourself. It's very hard to look at you if you are unsure of who you are and if you judge you as the enemy. You have always fought to be outside of you and now you are risking going within and claiming all those parts of you that you have never wanted to own or to acknowledge. You need help! You are not totally dysfunctional and you are not unfixable. You are simply moving from dysfunction into a more functional type of behavior. You are being moved out of what does not work for you into what will help you grow.

Many of you will hate this process. It will feel as though you are being stripped of your mask and facade. You will feel as though you are humble. You will find that you do not wish to be honest with yourself and so you play roles and act out parts. You do this because it makes you feel better about your "self." You have such a low opinion of yourself that you must create an image with which you can face the world with pride, or at least with some sense of dignity. Dignity is not something to be put on like a mask. You will learn to know yourself and to accept yourself as you are (with all your "faults" as you call them) and you will learn that you actually are a dignified being. You do have worth, value and promise. You are a Mercedes but you think you are an old beat-up pickup truck.

When you learn your value you will begin to shine. To get to your value we must take off anything that says "I am unworthy. I have no value." When you take off these layers you will "feel" them. This means that you will feel unworthy and worthless instead of valuable. Do not be afraid. This is a part of you that is going, it is no longer of value to you. You are going to value you more and more as you learn to let go of your old preconceived ideas of what you should or should not do in order to be acceptable to you.

*W*hen you become one with your own feelings you will be owning a big part of you. You have pushed out and pushed away your feelings all your life. This is taught to you early in childhood. If you say "I hate you" you are told to not say it or that you do not mean it. Hate is then negated and shoved away. If you cry, you are taught to stop immediately by many different means. It may be a pacifier in the mouth or a gentle soothing voice that convinces you that crying is not a good thing to do. You then grow up and when you want to cry you stop yourself. You push your true, natural feelings to sorrow aside and revert back to your training. You are all trained in your behavior and it does not allow room for natural feelings. This has caused a backup of emotions in the physical body which has suffered from being stifled. Now the body is beginning to reject the stifled emotions and you are all beginning to release them in various ways.

Most of you do not even realize what is occurring because you have been programmed or taught that if something does not feel good you should shut it off or push it away. Now "it" is in you and bigger and stronger than ever. "It" is built up energy that is waiting to explode or release. You may explode or you may consciously release what you hold in you. You may act out what is in you or you may simply stay calm and ride the feelings as they surface. The only problem with acting out is that you sometimes feel guilty after you have "acted" in certain ways. You may have remorse or feel out of control. I suggest that you consciously realize that you are discharging, and that you ride with the emotional currents and not get all caught up in it. This is why I say to not get involved and to breathe and stay calm. Hit your bed. Hit a pillow. Scream at a doll. Scream in your car. This makes it easier on you and for you.

When you begin to release so much "feeling" it will feel like you are drowning in your own emotions. You may feel "sick with fear" or "upset with anger" or "dying of sorrow and self-pity." Allow it! Flow with it. Ride it out. Do not be afraid to express your emotions to yourself and to allow them to show you where your wounds are. Do not be afraid to spend time with you working on you. Do not be afraid to take the time to be alone. You are all so afraid of being alone. You are never alone. There are so many you's that you could never be alone.

You will find that when you spend time alone you can focus more easily on you. You are the one who is searching for attention and you are the one who is in need of love, so I suggest that you give you some attention and some love. You all spend far too much time running from your feelings and not facing them. You hide and you withdraw and you try to control, because you cannot handle what you are feeling, and what you are feeling is pain. You are in need of a giant energy release to allow pain out of you and you need to discharge pain before it takes over your life. It is a cancer that is spreading in you and now we are going to release it by focusing on it. You will see how you use pain and how you have come to depend on pain.

For now I suggest that you not be afraid of what is in you and that you begin to allow it to express itself to you. Write down your sorrow and hate and hurt. Write it, and say it, and cry it, and kick it, and hit it, and get it up and out of you or you will put it someplace else. Maybe it will go into your spine and your back will give-out or hurt. Maybe it will go into your neck and your neck will get sore and you will get a headache. Maybe it will go into your legs and feet and you will cramp up or your knees will begin to bother you. It does not go away if you push it down "in you." You must begin to bring up your feelings and see what you really are.

Now; one of the ways that you will create to bring up feelings is to create a big trigger to release them. This could be in the form of a situation that you feel very uncomfortable in or a relationship where the other person pushes all your buttons. These situations either frighten you or cause you great stress. Look at why you are getting stressed. What is upsetting you and where does the judgment lie that has created the fear of this particular situation.

Everything is programmed in and can be programmed out. Release it and know that it does not have to be one way or the other. There are many ways and just because you strongly believe that your way is right does not mean that it is. You have been taught to see things a certain way and to judge situations as bad or not right. This programming is what you fall back on when you feel threatened by someone who doesn't think or act the way that you do. You begin to shift back into old attitudes and beliefs that say "this is good vs. this is bad." Now what you are learning is that good and bad are the same thing. It is all a perspective and if you name it bad it will become so and you will avoid it and fear it. If you name it good you will accept it and stay with it.

When you begin to release feelings you will begin to see how much of you is made up of judgment. You call everything wrong, or awful, or stupid, or not good enough. That is judgment. Your doubt in a person's ability to complete something is judgment. It is your judgment against you and it is how you see you. If you see others as not good enough or smart enough it is a reflection of how you see yourself. If you do not trust them it is a reflection of how you do not trust you. And if you do not care for them it is a reflection of how you do not care for you. You will find that everywhere you look, the only thing you ever really see is you!

*W*hen you first begin to see how your feelings are leading you in and out of situations, you will wish to secure your balance of uneven feelings. Most of you have feelings regarding every subject possible and these feelings are mostly taught to you by someone else who also had feelings about every subject possible.

When feelings get out of control and rush around, you tend to get out of control and rush around. You may want to stop rushing and begin to face your feelings. You may do this by consciously observing any situation that is pushing your buttons and try to see why it sets you off. What is it that makes you afraid? What is it that makes you want to fight this situation? What is it that upsets you most and how can you change your perspective so that you no longer are upset? When you begin to look at a situation in this way you will begin to see why your feelings are flying around and why you are upset by your feelings. You do not get upset by the actions of another. You get upset because you *believe* something wrong is occurring. When you begin to see how it is just your "point of view" you may wish to change your point of view.

You are not only in a position to change how you view any given situation you are also in a position to see all life from joy and to allow everything to occur as it does. When you allow everything to occur and you stop judging it as wrong or bad you will begin to slip into the flow of creation. When you slip into the flow you begin to see how you are guided in and out of certain situations in order to teach yourself who you are. Do not hold on. Do not stop the flow by not moving with it. Be a part of it by observing and allowing. Give up fighting and struggling to make things work out. Allow things to work out or not to work out. In this way you will be allowing all possibilities and you will be trusting in God and you will be trusting in you.

You will decide what is good or bad in any given situation because you have been taught to decide or to choose between good and bad. What if you had not been taught that certain things are bad? How would you "feel" about them and would you react so strongly as you now do? Would you get so upset when you "believe" that you are getting bad treatment? Would you look at everything as a shortcoming or would you begin to see the "gift" in all situations and experiences that occur?

Once you begin to look for the gift you will find it. You always find what you are looking for. If what you look for is danger you will find danger. If what you look for is pain and struggle you will find pain and struggle. You are not here to be in pain. You are here to learn to love and in order to love, you must look for love. Do not look for fear or misguidance and you will not find it. So many of you do not trust your own guidance and you are banging your heads against the wall trying to figure out what you have done wrong. Try to figure out what you have done wrong and you will find wrong. Do not look for wrong. Look for love. Be you and know that you are being guided and know that you are not being bad. You are good. You are love.

Be good by allowing you to be considered good! You only allow for bad. Do not judge how you are. Be you and trust that you are changing and growing and evolving and everything is in perfect order. You do not need to worry that you made a wrong turn and went the wrong way. There are no wrong ways and there are no wrong turns. Be who you are and love who you are. Allow you to be where you are and you will stop judging every situation as undesirable. You are turning off to life by calling it bad for you. You will wish to turn on to life by calling it good for you. Look for the good. Trust you. Trust God.

※※

When you begin to see how you are creating everything that occurs in your life, you will begin to understand the process of healing. Everything is an attempt to heal. Every situation that you create for yourself is for a reason. Do not overlook what you are creating. Do not close your eyes to your good work. You are seeing pain where you could be seeing joy. You are judging where you could be accepting. You are struggling where you could be flowing. You are so afraid of not getting good that you push good away. You are so afraid that you will be mistreated that you push at others until you are mistreated or until they no longer feel accepted by you. You will learn that you are all in pain and no one is exempt. You all create pain and confusion and then you blame one another. It is okay to feel like you are falling apart and it is okay to be in your pain. Do not put it on another and do not blame you for it. Allow it to be and see what happens when you acknowledge that you are the owner of your pain and you were riding it to see how deep it goes.

If you begin to concentrate on certain aspects of your life you might be able to see how you decided that pain was best. Some of you even hurt yourself before anyone else gets a chance. This is more or less self punishment and it comes from being so defensive that you allow no opening for positive action. You are so certain that you will get hurt that you block everything from coming at you. You even block love. You block all energy as you are protecting yourself from pain. So now you keep out joy, and peace, and love, and bliss, and health, and happiness. Your "well-being" depends on all of these and yet you have such a need to defend yourself that you block everything that comes at you. *You do not trust.* You do not trust that you will be loved and you do not trust that you will receive good. You are programmed by past experience to believe that only bad things happen and so you spend all of your time looking for the bad and allowing nothing else to be seen. "Look for the good!" Know that everything that comes into your life will be a big gift. Look for the gift until you find it.

Be aware of your ability to change good into evil. Be aware of your ability to see what you want to see. Be aware of your ability to distort what is really going on. Look only for the good in every situation. Do not judge it and do not judge yourself for drawing it and do not judge those who are taking part in the drama with you. They are simply acting out a role in your play. You are the director and you are creating chaos where you could be creating peace and love. You create it by visualizing it in any given situation. Stop visualizing pain and it will cease to be. Begin by visualizing good and by visualizing love and by seeing yourself receiving nothing but good. I don't care if you lose your job or if you lose a lover. These can be very good things. You were so strongly taught to hold on to things and people, and this inhibits you from moving on. Do not hold on. Let go and let God be in control. Stop judging what is occurring and you will begin to see how you may begin to enjoy what is going on in your life.

As you begin this process of letting go and allowing, you will begin to feel free of your need to "figure out how to make things work." This is a big problem for all of you. The question is always "should I do it this way or should I do it that way," and "what's best," or "what will get me the results that I want?" Let go of this form of struggle and begin to allow creation to work for you instead of knocking yourself out trying to do the right thing in order to get you what you think you want. You don't know what you really want. You are confused and misinformed and programmed to behave a certain way. We are creating a new way and it has little to do with where you have been, as we are moving into your future. Heaven is coming to earth. You may tune-in to heaven and peace or you may stay tuned-in to hell and the confusion it has.

*W*hen you begin to see how you are releasing your hold on how you feel about certain situations, you will be allowing yourself to see the truth in all its glory. The truth is that you do not need to hold on to feelings of pain. You are going to learn how you create pain in a situation just by feeling unsafe, or unwanted, or unneeded. When you feel unwanted or unappreciated you begin to push to gain acceptance. You begin to try harder to gain attention and recognition. This is due to your programming.

As a child you probably learned about competition. Whether it was in school or at home among your siblings, competition is always strong in your lives. You are now learning to let go of competition and to be who you are. Once you begin to accept that you need not be superior to others you will begin to release your need for this type of competition. You are playing a game to get attention because attention is energy, and you seek energy from outside of yourself simply because you are draining your own energy by hating you so much. Once you can learn to accept you and love you, you will no longer need to search for attention outside of yourself. Pay attention to you and you will be okay. Do not deny you and do not be afraid of who you are.

As you begin to release more and more of your own love power you will begin to "feel" more and more love in your life. You will actually begin to feel accepted and loved without a struggle. This will be when you have come into balance and you have been centered long enough to support being free of fear. Fear has a very strong hold on you and you have a very strong hold on fear. Basically, you believe what fear tells you and you forget what love tells you, so I will remind you. Fear says, "I am hurt, the world is a dangerous place," and, "you cannot let go or you will lose." Love says, "Yes, I feel good," and, "the world is my playground," and "I can let go of anything and always get more." You are not here to create from fear; you are here to create from love. Love is who you are and love is who you wish to be. Let go of fear ways and turn to love ways. When you love, you flow and you are at peace. When you fear, you block and you are upset. It is very easy to know if you are in love or fear. Blocked and upset is fear, open and flowing is peace and love. Once you begin to recognize where you are you can change where you are.

Now; when you begin to see how you are in fear you can easily switch to love by simply changing your mind about how you wish to feel. You may say, "I wish to experience love instead of fear" and you may say, "I am love and not fear." This will assist you in speaking to all parts of you who are involved in this process of transformation. Once you switch to love you might experience joy where you previously experienced pain. If this process does not work for you then I suggest you reread Book Eight through Book Fifteen to assist you in getting the old blocked pain up and out of you. Once you have released enough pain you will be ready to begin the change over from fear to love on a conscious daily basis. It is not necessary for you to constantly walk around with a big smile pasted on your face in order to feel love. Love will come in and change your hurt feelings to happy feelings and you will automatically be happy enough to smile. This will not take effort on your part. It will simply begin to occur.

As you begin to notice these types of occurrences you will also begin to see how you have grown more and more in love and less and less in fear. You are walking away from a very destructive relationship with fear. You are walking into a very healing relationship with love. This is how you "move" from one side of you to the other. You take the time to learn about you and then you take the time to understand you and then you take the time to be alone with you and allow you to transform. Once you can tolerate being "alone" you can tolerate you. You are the one who is with you all the time and if you are so afraid to be alone it is because you do not want to be stuck with you. You will find that the more you love you the more tolerance you will begin to feel towards yourself and towards others. If you cannot tolerate them it is because you cannot tolerate you. You are important to you so I suggest you learn how to tolerate you and to be very, very nice to you.

୭ଲୁ৶

When you are alone with you, you will feel as though you are not doing what you should. There is pressure in your society and culture to join and to mate. If you want to be alone you are called unsociable, or unfriendly, or no fun. You may find that you feel that there is something basically wrong with you if you do not require the company of others. You are not wrong to be alone and you are not wrong to be without a mate. It is okay to stay alone and it has nothing to do with your ability to receive. Not everyone makes the same choices and to be alone is a valid choice. You may find that you are more at peace or you may find that you enjoy the quiet of being alone. This may continue for a long time or for a short time. It does not matter and it is up to you. Those of you who do not know how to survive without someone to love should not criticize those who are less needy in that area.

When you begin to discover all of your patterns you will find that you often prefer to do what society says so that you do not look like you are doing what is not acceptable. Many marriages have been held together by society's belief that it is best to mate and have an ally. This leads one to believe that the struggle to survive is so great that you must depend on others for your spiritual livelihood. As you begin to see how you create the struggle you will begin to let go of your belief that you must have someone to assist you at all times. You are not in need of assistance but you are in need of self-esteem, self-love and self-control. You will find that these come from the self and they are part of the self.

When you begin to see how you can change your entire world by changing how you see it, you will begin to see how self-sufficient you really are. The days of needing a mate to populate the (your) world are over. The world is full of people and a majority of them are unhappy and suffering. Why make more? When you learn to shut off your need to procreate and leave part of you behind you will begin to reassess your *need* for a mate. You once bred and raised children to assist in working the fields and because religions told you not to use abortion. You have gotten so confused that you do not know why you do things. You are raised believing that your job is to grow up, marry, and have children of your own. Why? Do you ever question what you were programmed to do or do you just continue the cycle? Grow up, get married, raise a family. Why?

You will find that you have a lot of beliefs that have created a world that you no longer feel safe in. You feel out of control and, in some cases, afraid of your mate or even afraid of your own children. The children are afraid of you and all of life, so the cycle continues. You will begin to see the benefits of stopping and reevaluating some of your customs. For now, I just wanted to bring up a few for you to think about.

❧

When you first begin to clean out your subconscious you will be feeling your pain. Your pain is stored *in* you and may require some pretty big triggers to get moved out of you. You are in a healing process when you begin to let go of your pain. You will find that releasing pain is a painful process. This is due to the fact that you are being closed off from your true self by the storing of pain in you.

Once you begin to release the pain you may find that it has a great deal of charge on it or in it. This may be anything from emotional upset to mental anguish. As the pain leaves you, you will begin to re-experience those situations that cause you pain. This is different for everyone. What is painful for one person may actually be ordinary for another. If you are accustomed to being treated a certain way it will not upset you. If you are, all of a sudden, treated differently it may cause great upset. This is due to the fact that you require so much outside validation to maintain your belief in who you are. When you are no longer validated as the great worker, or good mother, or loving father, or kind person that you believe yourself to be, you may begin to get upset and no longer know who you are. It is like losing something and you all hate to lose. You hate to lose because you have been taught to win. You hate to lose because you think losers never win. You hate to be a loser.

It is very difficult to transform into a new being when the old being is holding so tightly to identity. You must let go of identity in order to shift to a higher level or perspective. It is most important to be who you are and, right now, who you are is changing. You are becoming much more than what you ever were before and, in order to become more of what you are going to be, you must let go of a few things that make you who you were or who you are now. You will *shift* and change and grow with everything you let go of. This may feel like struggle to you as you have never before been shown how to let go in order to move forward. You only know how to get promoted to more money or more things in your life. No one ever said, "Congratulations, you've just lost all your money."

It is scary and frightening for you to lose all your money. You will find that, more often than not, you will become much more successful when you have lost a few things. I know this is inconceivable to you but it is what occurs when you are evolving spiritually. You will also find that your pain is mostly centered around losing. Whether it is around fear of losing your life, or your children, or your boat, or your car, or your home, you fear loss and loss brings the pain it carries forward with it. It may not feel good but you will learn that, in loss, you receive your greatest movement forward. This is simply due to the fact that your greatest fear holding you back is fear of losing.

As you begin to clear greater and greater amounts of fear you will begin to recognize fear. How many of you, as you were reading the last paragraph on loss, were uncomfortable and felt like you did not believe it or did not want to hear it? How many thought, "Oh no, I'm going to have to give up something?" This is your fear of giving up and it is very, very strong. When you do begin to give up and release your hold on outdated ideas and beliefs you will be creating a very big void within you which can then be filled with a positive instead of a negative. The reason for reprogramming you is to create positive and release negative. If you can view your life in a positive manner you will be free to see how you are in love with life no matter what is going on around you.

I know that from where you are now you cannot comprehend this type of attitude but it is possible and it is a true state of love. When you learn to let go of what you are holding on to you will be in the flow and you will easily move on to love. When you continue to hold on to where you are because you like what you have, you will not move into the flow of love, you will stay where you are which is blocked in fear. I call it the "fear trap" you usually call it hell.

༄༅

*W*hen you begin to see the benefits behind knowing how your pain is held in you, you will be in a position to know more about yourself. You will also be in a position to love yourself and to grow into those areas of yourself that you have been pushing away. If you deny a part of you by not wanting to accept that it is you, you will be leaving that part of you. The idea is not to leave or abandon parts of you. You must learn to move into all parts and to be all parts. You may do this by accepting all parts and by knowing what you have done. You may have decided that to think a certain way is evil and so you shut down a part that was sending messages that you could not accept. You may have found that parts of you enjoyed some situation that was expected to be awful and maybe even judged as awful. If you enjoyed it you too must be awful.

You are now beginning to see how you are made up of many beliefs regarding many situations. You are beginning to see how you are not only not who you thought, you are far beyond anything you dreamed. When you begin to explore your own depths you will discover that you are much more than what lies on the surface. You think you are one way when, in actuality, you are another. You actually believe things that you have no idea or clue that you believe. You are creating out of belief and yet you do not have a clue as to what you really believe or who you really are.

As more and more parts of you begin to emerge, you will be astounded at how you have been in you all this time and yet never known you. You will also be amazed at how you can transform without shutting down. Once you learn how to let "you" out of hiding and to let you express your true nature you will feel much better. You will be freeing up big chunks of you and allowing them to surface.

One of your best measures of how you are doing is your ego. If you think you are right you probably are lying to yourself in order to protect yourself from the truth. The truth is that you are never right and there is no right. Whenever you make yourself right you make someone else wrong. You have been programmed very strongly to stay "right." If you are wrong you are bad, or stupid, or ugly, or any other such belief. So at all costs you project your rightness and your knowledge and your wisdom, and you are usually very proud of your rightness. Well, from now on I want you to be wrong. Find out how you are being right and let go of it to the extent that you can say to yourself, "I was wrong. I must be getting better." When you can accept your humanness and your vulnerability you can accept your true identity. You will be allowed to accept that you do not "know it all to be just one way." You will be allowing "all ways" to exist.

When you begin to change from being right and smart and on-top-of-it to being human, you will have made a giant shift within. You will find that, not only are you giving others around you a break from your "right ways," you are also giving you a much needed break. It is very tiring to always be the smartest one with all the answers and it is very tiring to try to figure everything out, especially when you don't even know who you are or what you really believe.

☙❧

You will begin to see how your feelings are attached to anger and pain. Everything need not be turned into pain. You can learn to see a situation and not get all emotionally charged by it. It may occur in your life to show you something about human nature and it need not be taken seriously or with pain. You may learn to experience pain or joy in your life. You choose in every situation how you will view the situation and it is up to you to take responsibility for your action and for your response to any given situation. If you choose not to respond from anger and self righteous behavior you will be choosing the road less traveled. The path of least resistance is always the wisest choice. Going with the flow is easy to say and not always so easy to do.

When you learn to be true to yourself you will be learning the greatest gift of all. You will be learning to be who you are and not who others wish you to be. To be your own self is often not what you have chosen in the past. To be your own self is to be love and understanding, because unconditional love is what you are and understanding often comes with unconditional love. As you learn to accept yourself you will be learning to accept your feelings. Feelings are very important. I know you all run around talking about how this person said awful things about you and that person did this to you, but basically it is all you. You create it in order to experience it, in order to learn by it. I suggest that you begin to learn to feel your own feelings without blaming them on everyone else. No one is awful unless you believe in awful. If you believe in awful then I suggest you let go of that belief.

As you learn to accept you more and more, you will be learning to accept others. When you stop judging you as awful you will no longer see others as awful. If *you* hurt your feelings it is all your doing. Do not point at others and scream how he or she did this or that to hurt you. Only you

I and God are One

can hurt you, so I suggest you begin to mature in the feeling department and allow yourself to learn to grow beyond the pain that *you* constantly seem to create for yourself. Remember, when you change pain to joy you are the one who gets elevated. If you blame your neighbor for your pain you will not get the results because you are giving away your feelings and your power.

Own your feelings by taking responsibility for them. You have been learning how to speak your mind and now I want you to speak your peace. Peace comes from taking responsibility for what you feel. You don't call another an idiot for being who they are. You simply learn that in allowing others to exist you are allowing you to exist. You are also allowing you to be free of judgment. You see, you would never have the ability to see another as an idiot if you did not strongly believe that you are an idiot. You can only project onto others what you carry. The more you hate about yourself the stronger your feelings of dislike will be for another who mirrors to you those qualities that you hate in you. Stop blaming the mirror for sending back the message that you sent out in the first place. You are big enough now to start taking responsibility for your own feelings. You may stomp around the planet and put things "right" and put people in their place by telling them how awful they are or you can stroll through life with peace and little effort. The choice is yours and it always has been.

47

You will begin to understand the dynamics between male and female energy when you have brought your own male and female essence into balance. Most of what you are viewing as male energy is actually aggressiveness and what you view as feminine is actually weakness. You provide definitions for masculine and feminine based on strength. This has created imbalance within society and within races and within your own inner essence. You have a battle within between strong and weak. You do not wish to be strong because you do not wish to harm another and yet you do not wish to be weak because you do not wish to be harmed. You have created polarities that are as far apart as any can get and yet they are right here inside of you. You are fighting inside of you. You have been fighting inside of you since you first began to create male and female polarities.

When you begin to see how this struggle within has created struggle without or outside of you, you will begin to get a better idea of how you are being kept in war and out of peace. You began to learn how to play a role and how to be a man or a woman. In playing the role you are encouraged to not cross over into the opposite role. Boys are strongly encouraged not to cry or to show emotions in public. Well, actually it's okay for them to fight and that's even admired, especially if they are fighting to protect their family or their honor. You can get medals for killing if you are a man. I realize that women are going off to war in several areas of the world, but, for the most part, it has been the male role to play fighter and strong one. It is the female role to get upset and express emotions through tears. This would never do for a man. You must control your fear and bring up your anger to look tough.

So; men and women have these roles that they are playing. Sometimes they get tired of their role and switch roles because they want to break out of the mold. This is done in various ways and you have tried to do the same thing within you. Sometimes you get tired of playing male/masculine/tough guy and you want to be female/feminine/soft guy. Other times you get tired of playing female/feminine/soft girl and you want to play male/masculine/tough girl. You all switch back and forth trying to figure out which is going to work for you. I would like you to know that you will come into balance and begin to walk in the middle. You will no longer feel the need to show your strengths nor your weaknesses. You will simply be at peace within you and so you will walk the middle road and no longer fall into macho-ism nor feminism. You will be human at last. You have tried for so long to figure out how to handle both sides of you and you are now beginning to merge both sides into one. Separation within will end and you will be whole.

When you have found your own balance you will know it. There will be no big turmoil in your life and struggle will end. Things will simply fall into place and you will have peace of mind. Did you ever have a day when something that would normally upset you didn't? All of a sudden you wonder why you're not upset. Normally you would be kicking and screaming but, all of a sudden, you just don't care anymore. This happens often in the letting go of things. Anyway, it will be symptomatic of all areas of your life. You will not get upset because you will just let go of your anger and control. You will no longer feel the need to control how everything is done either at home or at the office. You will have shifted from struggle into peace.

❧

As you begin to discover your own feelings you will unload all that has been hurting you. You have been struggling with your pain and your hurt and this is why you get upset when certain situations occur in your lives. For the most part you are being relieved of your pain in order that you might replace it with joy. When you begin to uncover your hurt and all of your hurt feelings, you will find that you also uncover your joy. Your joy has been buried along with your pain. When you shut down parts of you, you inevitably shut down other parts and you begin to lose big pieces of you in the process. When you regain your hurt you will inadvertently regain your pleasure. Pleasure and pain are very closely connected and they are buried in you together. The more pain that you can release and bring forward, the greater the opportunity for you to feel pleasure. You will find that not only are you pleasure, you are also pain. Do not be afraid to experience emotional pain. You are trying to cut it off by not feeling it and it is often pushed down deeper in you.

As you begin to discover how you may trigger and release by bringing yourself into certain situations, you may decide that all situations are not so painful as you once thought. You may even begin to enjoy the capability of release. To release what is trapped in you will begin to feel like relief and you will wish for more. The most beneficial types of release are those which are nontoxic to others. It is best to release in a fashion that will allow you to be free of your charge without attaching that charge to another. When you act-out or project onto another you lose the opportunity to take responsibility for the hurt. If you project your hurt onto someone else you focus your energy *against* them and you create an enemy or villain. Then you are right back in the cycle of victim/villain, good guy/bad guy, evil vs. good.

As you learn to take responsibility for your own pain you will be learning to see how you *allow* yourself to be hurt. Some allow little things to hurt or upset them. Others project big things out onto others. When you project your stuff onto another you are allowing that person to take responsibility for your feelings. You want to own your own feelings. You do not wish to have someone else walking around in charge of how you feel. You are feeling how you do about a particular situation or person because your buttons are being pushed. Look at what fear buttons are being pushed and you will know why you are creating a villain in someone else.

You may begin to let go of all villain/victim situations and eventually you will no longer struggle because you will no longer be at war. War ends without an enemy. You create enemies to fulfill a need. Let go of your *need,* and your war with the world or life will begin to cease. You are just now at a turning point. You may drop your guard and put down your defenses and go with the flow, or you may continue to protect you at all costs and this will continue to create enemies. Without an enemy there is no need for protection - protection against what?

You create the need for protection and now I wish you to create a need for unconditional love. Give it a try and see how it feels. You will find that most love is actually awareness that is turned into understanding, and understanding that is turned into caring or sympathy. When you create sympathy you create a very strong emotion. You then raise money out of sympathy in order to assist the sick and diseased. Now I want you to raise love; true, unconditional love out of your understanding. Give up on sympathy and wanting to help by fixing every situation, and begin to heal by loving every situation. This is a lot for you to think about, but you will do well once you move into your feelings because out of feeling comes understanding.

As you begin to go into your feelings you will find that you will feel many different emotional ups and downs. You will also feel many things that are simply boring or not as far up or as far down. This is all part of the process. You do not just carry pleasure and pain. You also carry moods, and mood swings, and all that goes along with every possible mood that you could be in. When you begin to release your emotions you begin to set them free. As your emotions begin to free themselves you will begin to notice a change in how you respond to life and to certain situations. You will begin to see a change in your patterns and you will begin to release what no longer serves you.

As you change, you will begin to notice that you are no longer living in fear. You have begun to leave fear behind and you have begun to move forward into love. At first you will only notice how you no longer worry about this or that, then you will begin to see how you are actually moving along in your life with little to no pain. Then you will begin to see how pain has left you and how you are replacing pain with joy and pleasure. Do not get confused when you begin to feel pleasure. It is not wrong to feel pleasure. You may find that your pleasure comes in spurts or you may find that it stays with you for days. Once you open to pleasure you open to love. Love and pleasure are in the same area of feeling and joy is there also. Once you begin to feel pleasure you are on your way.

When you begin to realize the power of pleasure you will not wish to go back to pain. You have two problems where pain is concerned. One is that you are very attached to pain as a source of motivation and two is that you use your pain to move you into anger. If you operated without anger you would not get all pumped up and hot about certain situations. You use your anger to burst out of situations much as a car uses extra fuel to thrust foreword or backward. You must stop using anger and pain as your fuel and begin to use pleasure and joy. Your life will be a great deal more rewarding and you will no longer suffer, as there is no suffering when you are using pleasure. Pleasure has the same effects as fuel. It can move you forward and backward. Pleasure is not so painful and it will last longer. You will find that pleasure does not hurt and it does not create chaos. Pleasure creates joy and joy leads to bliss.

As you begin to move from pain into pleasure you will begin to see how you create pain and how to let go of thoughts that create pain. This will give you the opportunity to switch whenever you feel yourself beginning to create pain. You simply stop how you are thinking and begin to "see it differently." This comes with practice and will be very easy for you once you have brought the majority of your pain and illness to the surface. You cannot show ill will towards others if you have let go of your illness. You have created illness to show you how to stop, look, listen and turn things around. So now you have decided to finally stop, look, listen and turn things around. You are turning you around. You were headed in one direction and now you are headed in another. The pleasure path is not as well-known as the painful path, but I'm certain you will enjoy (with the emphasis on "joy") it.

When you begin to wake up to the fact that you have big chunks of you that are asleep, you will find that you are in a struggle. Part of the struggle is due to the fact that you have been programmed to shut off parts of you and you continue to do so. You are now learning to accept you and to allow all parts to simply "be." This will be an entirely new experience for you since you often shut down the parts you do not like or do not understand. If it does not fit into your mode of what is good or right for you, you begin to shut it down. Now you are learning that you do not know what is good for you and therefore you do not know what to shut down and what to allow. And as you grow more and more accepting and less and less fearful, you will relax and allow more of you to exist. This is a good thing and it will allow you to see more of you. It will also allow you to know more of you. You may believe that you know you now but you do not.

As you grow in consciousness you will grow in expanded awareness. This will allow you to stretch. Now; I do hope you remember that each and every time that you stretch you then contract a little to accommodate the new releasing that is brought forward by the stretching. Did you ever notice how much nap time a child needs? It is because they are stretching and growing and it requires rest in between. Now you are stretching and growing and you will require rest in between. When you begin to shift in new directions you often require more stamina. This creates a big draw on your energy sources and you begin to use up stored energy. When your stores of energy are depleted you then begin to rest in order to create new cells and new places within you to live.

You see, you are opening you up so that you might be all of you instead of just part of you. You are beginning to shift into you and to become all that you are. Most of you have never really been in you. You have created a system whereby you are partially gone or partially conscious. This is all changing now and you are beginning to enter you. As you begin this entry process you will be stretching you. You will be filling you up in places that have been void or empty. This takes a great shift within you and it allows you to take in more light, as your true essence is light. You are a light being and you are beginning the shift from darkness to light; from unconsciousness to consciousness.

When you begin to see how you are accomplishing this shift you will have an entirely new view of yourself and your world. This shift will come in very gradual ways and it will be well worth the effort you put out. You will no longer struggle to come into you and you will no longer struggle to push out parts of you due to judgment placed on these parts. When you begin to accept instead of reject, you will be accepting you instead of rejecting you. This will feel very good and very calming for you. It will be the end of a very long battle within. It will be the end of the struggle between fear and love. It will not be that love has won over fear. It will be that fear has moved to its right place and love has moved to its right place.

There really is space available for all parts of God. Nothing need cancel out anything else. Everything has a job and a place and a purpose. Nothing is bad and nothing is good. If you were to look at the engine of your car you would not say, "This is bad and is not needed to run my car." All parts are necessary and it is just a matter of having them connected properly and in the proper place to do their job. Darkness has its place and its job. It is not evil and it is not bad. Stop pushing stuff away because you believe it to be bad. Live and let live! Let all parts of you live.

∾⟐∾

As you begin to release all of your built up charge against evil, you will begin to feel better. This is due to the fact that you are the one you are calling evil. You don't realize this yet but since you carry all emotions (hatred included) you *are* what you label as evil. You are bad because you feel hate and revenge and you even have a desire to kill. Some of you may not express this desire but you can be certain that it is in you. You have called certain behavior patterns evil and so you have created an evil part in you. You have labeled so many things as bad that you are having a hard time finding anything good. You are telling yourself that to feel certain emotions is dangerous so you shut off these emotions in order to be good and do things right.

Now you are stuck in a situation where you have judged you into a deep, dark hole. Now is the time to come up out of that hole by acknowledging that it is natural to have the desire to kill to survive. It is also natural to want to lie to cover up what you fear and it is natural to want revenge against anyone who has harmed you. The reason I say it is natural, is due to the fact that you have been programmed to behave in this manner. Anyone who is programmed to behave a certain way will usually do so to some extent.

Some part of you knows! Some part of you knows that you have the ability to kill and to rob and to lie and to cheat. You are so afraid of this part of you that you keep it hidden and you do not allow it to surface. Now is the time to bring it to the surface and face it. Allow your hatred to come up in you so that you do not go down with it. Allow your ability to kill to surface so that you do not die with it. I am not suggesting that you go out and kill someone. I am telling you that you know how to kill and you have created denial to protect yourself from the part of yourself that has the desire to kill. Anyone can be taught to kill. It's very easy to learn to act on impulse as you are seeing in your world today. Do not suppress what is alive in you. Admit it and feel it and know it. You may find that you cannot admit to such a horrible thought as you taking the life of another, but I assure you that you have in past lives, and some part of you is now so civilized that you will not admit that you are capable of such acts.

This is why you suppress you and try to keep parts of you down. You know what you are capable of and you do not trust you enough to let all of you express. You are afraid of you and how you will respond in certain situations so you avoid those situations. You do not trust how you will act-out what you feel so you suppress certain feelings and never let yourself know what or how you really are. This is how some of you have created what you call multiple personalities. You can't handle knowing what part of you thinks and feels so you shut that part off and begin to live in the part that you can handle. You are afraid of you. You have shut out and shut off many parts of you.

When you begin to return to you, you will begin to recognize yourself in others. You will become more of yourself and, in doing so; you will be capable of seeing more of you in another. If you have a real big problem with people who kill, it is your reflection of how big your fear of this part of you is. If you have a big problem with people who cheat and steal it is a reflection of how large your fear of that part of you is. Those who scream the loudest about injustices committed by others have the biggest fear of their own ability to be unjust, and so they put down others in hopes of putting down their own fear of their own capabilities. You are all made the same and you all fear you. You have created evil by believing that something outside of you creates. You call it the devil; I call it fear of self.

Love yourself enough to be honest with yourself and you will find peace. When you stop fearing your own capabilities you will have the opportunity to use all parts of you and to heal all parts of you. You are not evil and parts of you are not evil. You just got so confused that you shot your own foot, and now you call you a killer and so you hide the part of you who knows what you have done. Let all parts come to the surface and when they do, do not judge you for being human and containing the full range of emotions.

When you begin to see how your feelings are directly connected to your beliefs you will see how you can change your beliefs in order to change your feelings. If you want to feel better, see things from a better perspective. If you want to feel happy wear a happy perspective and believe happy, positive thoughts. If you cannot force yourself to do this now it is because the joy is stuffed too far down in you and you must wait until you bring it out. Along with the joy will come whatever you buried with it. This could be hurt, or sorrow, or trauma depending on how you perceived and then received any given situation. When you begin to bring the trauma, sorrow or pain to the surface the joy will automatically follow. It is attached to sorrow. If something angered you or hurt you, you have sorrow. If you tried to push the sorrow away it went down in you and it took its opposite, which is joy, with it. Each time you push something away you push its entire spectrum away. Joy and sorrow are one and they act and move as one.

When you begin to raise your vibratory field you begin to jar loose all restricted emotions. You begin to free what is trapped in you and you begin to release what is trapped in you. Do not be afraid of the feelings that you are releasing. You will be allowed to move through them and, in so doing, release them. You may need triggers to get to the big stuff that is trapped in you, and you may draw situations that will assist you by bringing great fear to the surface in order to release everything that is attached to that particular fear feeling. As you release the fear you free the feelings. Some of these feelings are very "big" in you and you will tend to blow things out of proportion. Your fear will run amuk and you will feel out of control. This is good! It will not feel good nor will it feel like fun. You, however, will know that the trigger was created by you to assist you in your clearing and releasing, so that you might live in joy and not fear.

Be thankful every time you "feel your fear." You are so accustomed to pushing it away and when you push it away it has nowhere to go but back down in you and eventually it will bring you down with it. This is a time for rising up and, in order to do so, all parts of you must rise with you. Fear comes up to transcend its outdated role as the evil one. It is part of you and it is all blown out of proportion. We are bringing fear back into balance by releasing its hold over you. Fear is not the enemy. Fear is you. You are love and you are fear. We must get you to focus on both before we can get you to cross over to love. Let the fear out. Feel it. Know it. Realize that when you fear your feelings, you actually fear you. It is like fearing your right arm so much that every time it swings in front of you, you push it back behind you. This can, and has created problems. Do not push part of you away. Know you and you will know God.

❧

*A*s you begin to release your old buried charges you will find that you are full of beliefs that cause you pain. Once you learn how to tell the difference between what is painful and what is not, you will begin to feel your way to joy. As you open to feelings of joy you will find yourself in a new state of mind. You will no longer judge situations that once were considered to be bad. You will no longer be afraid of not being in control and you will no longer fear that you cannot trust you. This is the major issue. You do not believe that you can trust you and this is why you always watch out for, or keep your eyes open for danger. You are looking for bad things to happen because you are programmed to believe that only good people have good lives, and since you are a firm believer that you are not good, you "expect" bad. "Bad people lead miserable lives" - this is the programming. So, you decided long ago that you are bad and now you treat yourself accordingly.

I want you to begin to see yourself as good. No matter what you do, I want you to see it as good. I want you to begin to believe that you are good. You are and you know it on some level. That level is buried under the big lie that you have been subjected to since you were born into a body. That lie is that you can choose between good or evil. There is no evil, there is no such choice. Your standards of behavior have nothing to do with good or evil. They have to do with simple choices that affect you and others. To call a choice evil is ridiculous.

Now that you are beginning to see how you could possibly be good and even God, how can you judge anything that occurs in your life? You are moving into creation and you being created as you go. Stop judging your creation. Stop being afraid of making a mistake. Begin to see all life for what it is. It is fun and games. You came here to enjoy yourselves and somehow you got off track. It is time to bring out the joy and stop wallowing in your pain. It is time to begin to "feel your pain" so that you might release it. Do not be afraid to feel your pain. Allow it to come up in you and allow yourself to feel whatever is coming up in you. If you do not allow yourself to feel, how can you possibly feel joy? It is all a matter of knowing how you work. Feelings are keeping you safe by shutting down or shutting off. Now you are opening up and you will be allowed to feel free by allowing your unsafe feelings out.

When you have released enough built up charge you will feel freer in your choices because you will no longer be putting you down for your choices. Once you have taken in enough awareness or "light," you will begin to respond from awareness or light. Do not judge this part of you. This part of you will not act out like you do. This part of you will be forgiving and not hold a grudge. This part of you will say, "hello my friend" when you (ego) will want to snub your nose at someone who you believe to be bad or not good to you. This part of you is what creates love and self forgiveness. If you lose your edge and cannot snub another how can you possibly snub yourself? How can you ignore and put down others if you are no longer ignoring and putting down you? You cannot. What you do to others is simply a reflection of what you do to yourself. When you cannot snub or put down someone you hold a grudge against, you have begun to release the grudge you are holding against you for whatever bad thing you believe that you did.

⚜

You will find that you are among the very strongest of beings. You have adaptability and you have flexibility and you have choice. You are in a position to choose to heal and you are in a position to choose to be free of your programming. You may offer yourself more by choosing to give up more. You may also become more by allowing yourself to become aware of more.

You are in a position to become all that you are created for. You will find that you have been put in this position by the simple desire to be all that you truly are. When you desire God you get to be God. When you desire less you get to be less. You have found that you need only ask and you shall receive. In the asking is the power, your desire is what will set you free. If you desire to be rich you will get locked into ways of getting money. If you desire to be free you will be set free of your locked-in status. You will begin to circulate and to flow. If you are free you do not lock-in to any specific reality or belief. If you are free you can go anywhere and you can fit in anywhere. If you are free you can change direction at a moments notice and go the other way. Right now you are not free and it is very difficult for you to reverse your thoughts in order to reverse your direction.

Once you learn how you are locked in to a specific way of seeing any of your situations now occurring for you, you will begin to unfold your grip on doing it your way. I know you believe your way is best but that is only because you were taught to believe that. What if you were taught the opposite of what you now believe to be correct? Wouldn't it make perfect sense to do everything from the perspective of how you were taught? Well, now is the time to reverse your beliefs and begin to exchange them for ideas. Get out of "I have to do it this way" and get into "what if I did this or that instead."

You will begin to see that your beliefs are holding you in place and they are not shifting with you. Begin to consciously shift your beliefs. Begin to consciously allow yourself to react to every situation from a whole new perspective. Find humor where you would normally see pain and begin to see how everything is only what you make of it. You can make it awful, or traumatic, or terrifying, or funny, or enlightening, or just plain nothing. You give everything its meaning by giving it a label. If it feels funny you call it funny. If it feels tragic you call it tragic. Someone taught you to do this. Who were your teachers? Where were their fears? Are you not now them? You took on their beliefs and now you are like them because you see the world as you were taught by them to see it. You are creating cycle after cycle of belief patterns that are passed down from generation to generation. You may not act the same as your primary teachers but you are simply using their information in your own way. You may bend it and twist it to disguise it but you are still very much like those who taught you.

As you begin to grow out of your patterns and cycles, you will begin to heal. A pattern is a solidified way of doing things and it is your way of keeping what you believe. As you let go of what you believe, your patterns will begin to change. The only reason you do not break out of your patterns is because you believe you are right and being right keeps you stuck. As you begin to shift your beliefs, you will begin to see how "right" is something different for everyone. It depends on who you believe and what you believe. So; the big question is "what do you believe and who do you believe?"

*W*hen you begin to give up parts of yourself you will begin to see how you have been taught to believe in your own ways. Then, when something or someone comes along who is different from what you were taught, you decide that your way is right and their way is wrong. You will even find ways to support your belief and you will begin to see only what you want to see. This is how you become so afraid of moving outside of your tiny world and this is how you become "confined" within your tiny world. As you begin to release your hold on your limited perspective you will begin to see how you are not only 'not' being fair to yourself, you are very limited in what you can give to yourself. This is part of the reason that you do not wish to be in pain. You have limited the way you can "receive" to the extent that nothing feels good and everything feels bad. This, of course, is your classic style of looking for the wrong or bad instead of focusing on the good.

You are being stretched at this time. You are being taught to give up part of you in order to have more. You will not like the feeling of giving up part of you, even though the part you are giving up is the part that says, "No, this is not good enough. I deserve better." As you let go of this part of you, you will be allowed to see how you can have anything once you stop "judging" everything. Once you have let go of your desire to be free of your own good, you will be in a position to receive good. Yes, I said let go of your need for good. You stop everything and say, "This is not good enough for me," and you push it away. This creates big blocks to receiving and it allows you to see from a very limited perspective. Soon you will open to receiving and once you do I hope you can remember to continue to receive and to continue to stay open. Once you close down by judging every situation, it is very difficult to open you back up.

꿈

*W*hen you first begin to "rise up" out of your old way of viewing reality you will be seeing your own creations through new vision. You will be leading yourself into new areas of thought and acceptance of all that you create. Once you learn to accept and own all that you create you will automatically stop judgment against it. You will begin to know and to receive from your awareness. You will begin to awaken certain "thoughts" that have been dormant in you and you will begin to see how you have created and re-created things to show you who you are.

As you begin to see how you are creating very big gifts for yourself, you will find it unnecessary to continue to judge your life as bad. We will have switched you from track A to track B and your thinking will switch also. As you begin to move along in your thinking you will become aware of your cycle of patterns and how they affect your current reality. If you are stuck in a particular pattern it is to teach you how to grow beyond it. The best way to learn to climb a ladder is to start with a ladder. The best way to learn to rise above pain is to start with pain. You don't learn to climb a ladder by avoiding ladders and I will guarantee you that it is the same with pain. You do not learn to rise above pain by avoiding pain. Welcome pain by allowing yourself to feel why you are pushing it away. Now; I am not asking you to become a masochist or to begin to enjoy pain. This too is out of balance. I am, however, encouraging you to stop running from your physical, emotional and mental pain long enough to see it for what it is. Pain is a signal that something is wrong. When you begin to release your fear of pain you will no longer run from it as you now do.

At any given moment you are not above your density. Your density is what holds you down and it is composed primarily of one belief. "If I do this it will be wrong (or hurt me)." This is what keeps you safe in some cases and a prisoner of fear in others. You are all locked up with your fear and it has made you thick with it. I want you to go on a diet and to release some fear by going into your pain. What frightens you enough to cause emotional or mental pain? Would you consider going into your fears? Would you consider going into relationships or areas that feel uncomfortable? How would you like to walk hand in hand with God and take off some of your greatest fears? How would you like to be free of fear and insecurity, and to stand tall at any given time in any given situation; no fear, only love to guide you? You may do so by trusting God and by allowing only good to be in your life.

You allow good by knowing that nothing bad ever happens and by realizing that everything is created by divine order to get you where you are going. You may have your goals set and get very upset when they do not flourish or even bloom. It is not up to you; not this you anyway. It is up to God to decide how you will evolve and how you will rise up. You are God as well as many others. You have a great many masks that you wear and one of them is truly holy. You know everything and you know how to get you "up" and out of your fearful thinking. You are experiencing many changes in your life because change is good for you. Flexibility is good for you and letting go of "your way" of seeing things is very good for you.

⚜

You are now going to see how you can change. You are going to become more of your own self by allowing your programming to surface. This in turn will allow you to see what you have hidden from yourself and it will determine how you see yourself in the future. You are going to be using a great deal of energy and you are going to be using a great deal of sensitive monitoring. This will allow you to actually "feel" what you are doing. So often you act out and you think you are "right" but you do not "feel" how you are actually being stubborn. You will begin to "feel" and to allow your stubbornness to fall by the wayside. You will begin to yield and to give up your need to see it this way or that way. You will begin to see how you no longer will be in need of being right, and you will begin to see how you can have joy once you let go of your need to hold on to your rightness.

As you learn to become more and more flexible you will begin to see how you are being more and more lovable. It takes flexibility to accept and to allow the self freedom. This freedom comes from not wanting to control everything and it comes from being aware that you need not control to get your needs met. For so long now you have been programmed to control situations in order to not be cheated. Now I want you to be cheated. It is only in your mind that you will be getting cheated and soon you will find the gift. You are being put in position whereby you might let go of certain frailties in order to build strength. If you are cheated out of something it is good. It will strengthen you and it will allow you to see how much fear you have in this or that particular area.

Being cheated is a big fear for all of you. You worry about your spouse or lover cheating on you and you worry about getting cheated out of your fair share. This could be anything from a job assignment or position to a new home that is not quite what was advertised. You fear being overcharged for services and you fear being left out or left behind when it comes to raises at work. Being cheated is a very big fear that occupies more of your thought energy than you realize. You are so afraid of being made to look like a fool, and this is why you are so stubborn. You stand rigid and will not give when you believe that you are right. This is due to the fact that you believe others to be wrong and life to be unjust.

What if life were always just? What if you had a belief that everything occurred according to divine plan? Would you then dig your heels in and fight for your rights or would you flow with life and wait to see what the divine had to offer? Would you kick and scream about not being treated fairly by your boss or spouse or whomever, or would you simply "know" that everything was occurring in your own best divine interest? Would you then trust or would you continue to struggle to get "your way" and to get "your piece of the pie" - your "fair share" as it were? So; who is flowing in trust and faith today? Is it you? Are you going to go to work and complain about how everything is done or are you going to give yourself a break from the struggle and accept everything as divine order? How big are you? Can you be flexible enough to handle it?

❧

Once in awhile you begin to feel the shift in your body. This shift is taking place within all of your cells and, therefore, it is becoming part of your life. This shift in consciousness is moving you into a new area of your own beingness. You are becoming all that you can be and you are becoming all that God is. As you shift you will feel changes physically, emotionally and mentally. All parts of you are affected by this change or shift in perspective. The perspective was once on evil, and wrong, and awful, and bad. The perspective is now moving over to God, and good, and life, and understanding, and acceptance.

As you shift from blocking to allowing, you will no longer get hit with so much energy. When you block everything from your life you must put a great deal of energy into protecting yourself. Now you are going to trust that God is working in your life and that all is in divine order. This may be a bit difficult for you since you believe that you must protect and defend yourself at all costs. What if you no longer required defense? What if defense was what blocked you from receiving? What if you could receive if you would just stop blocking everything that came at you? You are so afraid to receive that you shut down receiving in favor of controlling. What occurs then is the freezing up of reception. You have blocked everything in order to keep you safe and now you have been frozen in the position of blocker. I want you to become a receiver.

When you learn how to let go of your position you will be flexible enough to move all the way across the line from blocking to receiving. Once you let go of positionality and no longer take a firm stance, you will be on your way. Those of you who have set ideas and set ways of doing things will want to uproot your ideas and let things be shifted to all positions instead of just one position. The best attitude is that anything is possible so why judge anything as not good. Do not label others as stupid or incompetent, for they are simply here to show you who and what you are. Allow everything to be okay. This means they all have a purpose and you just don't know yet what that purpose is.

As you begin to move further away from defense and closer to reception you will begin to feel a little off center. This is due to the fact that you have always been stuck in one way of seeing things and now you are moving into many possibilities. This is a very confusing time for you. You have lived your life based on right and wrong and now you are moving out of that particular belief system. How can you know what is good for you if you cannot label some choices as bad? This is how I wish you to move into your new, liberated, free thinking. You will first begin to realize that everything that comes to you is for you. You may learn and grow or you may push it away and scream about how unjust life is.

As you begin to receive and accept what comes to you, you may work to rise above your current limited way of seeing life. If you push away what has come to you, you create a struggle whereby you are actually stuck to what you are struggling or fighting with. When you push at it you actually touch it and, by so doing, you become part of it. You get involved with it and it gets involved with you. If you simply watch it and begin to see how you might rise above it by not getting involved in a pushing match, you will be able to see it differently and therefore make it different. You create everything you see into what it is for you by how you see it. Some of you love what others hate. You create it by your attitude towards it.

Once you learn to see how it is all you making your world up as you go along, you will begin to see how you are indeed the creator. You are also the created. You make you up as you go along by how you perceive your own self. You will learn how you literally create and change your perception of yourself as you go. You allow you to be by allowing you to grow in certain areas. You stifle you in areas that you do not trust and you flourish in areas you do trust. It is easy to see where your trust lies. There, is where you will find the greatest joy in life. If you do not trust, you do not venture forward. Once you learn to trust everything, you will have joy in everything. This simply means that you will no longer get upset about anything because you will know that everything has a good and divine purpose. This type of trust will bring on joy of life, which will allow you to put aside your fear and let your defense go. You will begin to see joy where you never thought possible. This is my promise to you. Joy is everyone's gift. You must let go of your defensive behavior so that you might receive it.

⚜

When you begin to see how you are no longer a part of evil you will begin to recognize how creation is good. All creation is good! You have no evil. You, however, will still try to label certain aspects of life as evil. This may be in order to protect yourself or it may be to become involved with what you label as evil. If you become involved with it you get to know it. If you get to know it, you sometimes can overcome your fear off it. When you do not overcome your fear of it you continue to label it as evil, and it will come back to you so that you might once again get involved with it and get to know it for what it really is.

Most of you do not fear evil so much as you fear the thought of evil. This allows you to become involved with evil thinking or evil acts that are thought about and discussed amongst you at great length. When you finish discussing evil and evil-doers you are usually pretty well afraid for yourself or happy that you do not have such evil in you. You, however, do not recognize what is in you, and your attempt to suppress evil or wrong on the outside is simply an attempt to continue to suppress your own inner workings that you fear as evil. Watch yourself. If you are working hard to put down evil in your world you are more than likely working on yourself.

You will find that as you go from one "state of being" to another you will shift out of fear and into love. If you shift to love then you will learn that evil is not evil and you will learn to accept what is destiny or the divine plan. As you learn to accept what *is* as the life cycle, instead of seeing it as punishment for not being good, you will begin to move into a whole new perspective on what is manifested into form. Fear can be manifested into form. You might have such great fear of authority that you manifest that fear into form. This could be something as simple as a traffic ticket or something big enough to land you in jail. It is your fear brought to the surface and projected forward so that you might release it. It will allow you to be free of your basic fear and it will allow you to get involved with authority to get over your fear of authority.

When you have manifested such a fear into form, it simply means that you are working on healing that fear so it has come to the surface. Each individual will get as involved or uninvolved as it takes for them to move through the basic fear. Some of you get so accustomed to fighting and struggle that you continue to fight and struggle with authority your whole life. Others give up and pay the price to authority to get out of conflict and struggle. Usually you are protecting something when you do not wish to give up. You might be protecting your life so you will not have to live in jail or you might be protecting your money so you will not have to pay a fine. Sometimes the fight pays off and you save yourself from going to jail or you get out of your fine. Either way you have won. If you go to jail or pay a fine you win. You have the experience of facing your fear and allowing it to surface. You have won.

When you begin to see how some manifestations are simply brought on to show you how you are, you will no longer fear the manifestation. You will see that you are capable of dealing with all aspects of yourself including the fear aspect. Each individual carries fear and will, at some point, be allowed to face certain fears in order to grow beyond them. This is not a punishment! Do not judge yourself for creating situations that will assist you in your growth. You are learning to rise above fear and to move up into love. You do not do this by simply turning a switch and saying, "Okay, all my fear is gone." You will manifest what you need to push your fear buttons so that you might *feel your fear.* You are not afraid to feel your fear, are you? You must learn to accept and allow all parts of you... even the fear.

⁂

*A*s you begin to see how there is no way you are going to 'not' experience growth, you will begin to understand how you are simply experiencing growth pains. As you begin to stretch into new directions you will feel this stretching much in the same way that you would feel sore after stretching a muscle that had never been used. You may become overwhelmed at times as you are being stretched to accommodate more light. You have lived so long in darkness that to allow for light is a very big stretch.

As you learn to grow in light you will feel the effects on various levels. You will not only enjoy more areas of your life you will also begin to expand into greater areas of thinking. As all of this begins to occur you will begin to feel exhausted. It is like going to school. You study and take on the vast amounts of information and then you must rest your tired brain. You will find that as you learn, you will also begin to change form. Your form is shifting as you are shifting. This may take a while to actually see, but it is beginning to occur as you stretch to take on more light.

Now; when you begin to observe certain changes in your body I wish you to know that not all of them will be pleasant - not at first anyway. You may begin to dry out and lose old skin and you may begin to see infection come to the surface, or even sores may appear. Do not fear. In time all will heal. This takes a little time and it is natural for unhealed places within you to come up to the surface as they are being released. It may take a year or more for big hurts to manifest physically and then fade away. Do not be upset if you see things appear on your skin. Your skin is the last layer between you and the outside world. You may wish to allow for healing naturally or you may rush to your doctor for help. Just know that prescription drugs are still drugs and they may have other side effects within your body.

As you begin to heal and then to stretch a little more, you will begin to get a rhythm going and you will begin to see how you may actually be changing and shifting and growing with the seasons. Just like nature you are connected to all rhythmic cycles. You are nature. You are natural except for the chemicals you inhale and eat. So, as you begin to shift with the rhythmic sway of nature you will find yourself right in sync with every part of nature. You are growing and so is nature. You are taking on light and so is nature. You are living on the earth and so is nature.

You are like a plant or an animal in that you are not only part of nature you are also part of God. You are part of the same cycles and you are part of everything and everything is part of you. To believe that you stand separate from nature is ridiculous and to believe that you stand separate from God is ridiculous. If you kill you, you will simply become something else. If you kill a plant it will simply become something else. It does not die and you do not die. Sometimes the other alternatives are not as pleasant for you, as you see them from a position of fear. If I were to suggest you become a rock you would not be too thrilled with that idea. This, of course, is only due to your low level of awareness concerning how it is to be energy.

As you shift and grow to new levels of light awareness, you will be less and less certain that you know what is best and more and more aware that everything is actually very, very good. Only you judge! No one else judges this plane but you. The animals do not judge it. They exist in it and work with it. You judge them as a lower form of intelligence than you - but are they? Who is smarter - the one who works with the cycles of nature or the one who judges everything? Who is more aware of what is going on - the one who instinctively knows or the one who has to try to figure everything out to make some sense of it? Do you really think you are above the animals just because you walk and talk and wear expensive clothes? You have a great deal to learn about existence and what existing is.

You will soon begin to see how you create all the drama, or lack of it, in your life. You will see how you decide what to call things and then they become what you are calling them. Say you have decided to take a few days off work and you are going to rest. You might just lie around and read or watch a few movies. You might also begin to write a diary or to clean out a few closets. To you this is time off just for you and you enjoy it tremendously. Your next-door neighbor may also decide to take some time off. He plans an exciting outing into the woods and is ready for camping. He has no idea that the weather is going to turn very cold and he will cancel his trip to the woods. Now, instead of camping out he is at home and miserable. He wants action and instead is forced to stay in out of the cold weather. There is nothing for him to do but watch of few movies or read. You go back to work and rave about your great, relaxing time off. Your neighbor goes back to work and complains about his boring time off. You each did the same thing. One loved and enjoyed the experience while the other did not. It is perception and the ability to enjoy where you are in any given moment.

Do not judge slow times in your life. They have their purpose and they allow you to gather energy for your next move. You are constantly moving and shifting and now you are learning to flow with this shift that is taking place. If you can learn to always flow with life you will be free-flowing spirit. You will be connected and yet not attached. Once you learn how to go beyond your immediate need to be in control, you will shift into acceptance of where you are now and you will stop trying to put you somewhere else.

As you begin to reconsider how everything has a purpose you will be seeing the good in absolutely everything. You will begin to understand how you can be led more easily through life if you stay calm and accept everything as an opportunity for growth. Even the slow, boring times are an opportunity for growth. You will rebuild and regenerate in those slow times. You are like a flower and you do have your dormant time. You will stretch and grow at certain times and then you will rejuvenate and burst open with vibrant colors. You do not just stay in one position. You have much to do and it is done in phases. We will call these phases "the phases of your growth."

You will find that the more rapidly you shoot forward in any area of growth, the more rest time you will require after this expulsion of energy. The energy expelled must be replaced. Rest is required for the cells to reproduce and re-enter new data. Once you clear a programmed trauma it must be replaced by new information. Each time you lose part of you by moving forward and letting go of old pain you must put something where the pain was. You don't want a hole in you so you require time for light to enter and rebuild the damage left by the old programming. If you have recently had a big shift in consciousness the same thing may occur. You are shifting and releasing old stored information that is no longer necessary. Now you find it going and it must be replaced with new data. This, of course, will be truth instead of lies and it will come in and make its home where the lies once were stored.

As you continue this type of shifting and maintaining growth of consciousness, you will be allowed time to heal and rest. Whether you know it or not you are exhausted on the cellular level. You let go of a big chunk of you in order to move into a new awareness. This causes exhaustion and the need for rest is increased. I have told you repeatedly not to worry if you sleep more. It is good. Everything is good. Look for good. Nurture yourself. Love yourself. Take real good care of yourself. And please remember that God is being born in you and you are nurturing God when you nurture yourself. God and you are one. Hug you and you hug God. Love you and you love God. Be with you and you are with God.

❧

As you begin to receive, you will begin to stretch. You cannot receive without being stretched to some degree. Most of your receiving will be accompanied with some sort of stretching to let in whatever it is you wish to receive. You will open in places that were previously closed and you will begin to see how you are no longer in a position to be the one who is in control. As you begin to receive, you will begin to lose control in areas of perception. Your idea of what is good for you is not necessarily what you will receive. You will be more likely to receive what God believes you need in order to evolve up the ladder to ascension. You will receive all that you require and you will learn to push your way to the top even though it does not feel like the top. You will find that once you are moving on an upward spiral you will become very grateful for your change of heart and your change of attitude. You will begin to see the benefit in being "open to receive" and you will not restrict this receiving to simply material goods and desires of the emotions.

As you learn to move more and more into your future, you will find that every time you stretch, you then contract. This contraction may follow directly after your expansion and it may feel like you have not gotten anywhere in your evolution. Once the contraction has subsided you will begin to feel the strength that was brought on by the original stretch. As you move through your fears you will contract and expand many times. Do not be impatient with this process. It is as natural as breathing in and breathing out. You will find that it allows you to clear and to release old programming without interfering too drastically in your life. You are moved or stretched forward and then you are allowed to rest and to regain strength and even to feel the loss of your old programming. Each time you move forward by letting go of some big trauma or hurt, you are releasing the "idea" that pain was inflicted upon you.

You do not require yourself to be in pain when you allow yourself to release or let go of your belief that pain was given to you. You must allow the "belief" and the reception of pain to be transformed, and you must see how you created any given event as a painful situation simply by judging it as such. Should you decide to let go of the pain altogether you must also release the original judgment that created the pain. Once you learn that it was simply a misguided call, or label, that you stuck or tagged onto a situation, you will receive by letting it go. This type of reception is the reception of awareness, which is when the light inside of you turns on. You say, "Oh my goodness, I could have seen and received that entire situation differently!" You then begin the grieving process. This is due to the fact that you have just let go of a big hurt that you have carried and nursed since you were little. The hurt has become a part of you and you are losing that part of you. In some cases you have nursed your old hurts to the extent that you actually love them as you would an unborn baby in your womb. You carry and nurture old hurts and wounds and now it is time to give them up and let them come out.

As you begin to see your old hurts resurface you will be allowed to view them from a new, enlightened and nonjudgmental standpoint. You will be allowed to shed your old wounds as though they were a heavy woolen coat that has kept you warm with its weight. The heat generated by pain burns hot and cold. You may be detached and no longer connected to your feelings or you may be very hot and upset and really attached to your feelings. As you learn to release both your attachments and your detachments you will be brought into balance. You will no longer run hot or cold. You will begin to run in the middle, and you will feel very warm and nice and cool at the same time. You will no longer find it necessary to get red-hot and angry in order to get your needs met and you will no longer find it necessary to grow cold in order to cut off others who are needy.

You will begin to walk the middle and you will begin to know a lightness of spirit. This lightness is part of your birthing process. Once the big coat, or weight, has been lifted off your shoulders you will walk with new lightness and you will no longer suffocate under its burden. As you take off your coat of pain I hope you remember to give yourself time to heal and adjust to no longer having pain. It is not comfortable for you to not have pain as you have always carried it in you. You will have some adjusting to do so please be patient and do not freak out and think you are losing. You know that you are losing but it is a necessary loss.

⚛

*W*hen you become one with your own beingness you will have reached your goal. Your goal has always been to be whole. When you are whole you are complete and you feel fulfilled. As you learn to grow in harmony with your own self you will be learning inner tranquility and peace. You will learn how to share your most unknown truths without pushing. You will learn how to allow your most unknown desires without acting out. You will also learn to come into balance.

As you reach this state of wholeness you will begin to discover a new view of reality and it will be this new view that will show you heaven on earth. As you begin to realize your own heaven on earth you will be free to stay or to leave. You will have free will as you now do and you will be allowed to remain in a state of bliss if you wish. When you decide to leave, you will know that you can always return. So; why would anyone leave a state of bliss? - you ask. Because they want excitement. Some of you require huge amounts of stimulation to keep you going; to keep you interested in life. You also believe that those who do more are more interesting.

As you learn to be whole you will also learn to see everything as less fragmented. The only reason that you see things as one-sided or partial is because you are lopsided and not whole. Once you become whole you will develop a more rounded view of reality. You will also develop a more positive view of reality. Negativity is something that grows and thrives in fragmentation. When you put all the parts of you back in place you will no longer be a breeding ground for negative thoughts and self sabotaging behavior. You will be well-rounded and, as you become whole, your thoughts become whole and less fragmented. As you begin to receive more and more of yourself into you, you will be replacing empty space with light. You are light. You are a light being and you are coming into you in order to live in you and make you complete. Creation is being created. It is being fulfilled. It is arriving at its end. You are 'becoming' and, as you do so, you are arriving inside of you to allow you to be born of God or born of light.

This is an ongoing process and it does not mean that you end - not literally. It simply means that you end being the fragment and you now become whole. Your world does not end - not literally. It too will end being fragmented and become whole. This is how stories of the end of the world are created. You believe you are ending and you actually are. So much is occurring that you are not consciously aware of. Cells are shifting and changing within you and you have no idea how significant these shifts are. As you learn more and more about yourself you will begin to "feel" more and more of the shifting. This will be due to the fact that you are more in tune with you. You are less separate from you. You are less fragmented and you are coming together as a whole.

As soon as you become whole your entire world will shift. You will be working and living from a much stronger power base. Anything that is whole and complete has great strength. It is much stronger than anything that is fragmented. When you are fragmented you are going off in all directions and you are incomplete. Once you become whole you are headed in one direction and you have purpose. As you learn how to determine your purpose you will learn how to know why you have decided to be created. When you learn why you decided to be created you will gain insight into the simple act of creation and how you all use it. You create you. You ask to be born and then you are born. You become personality and then you change personality. You take on roles and then you drop roles.

You do it all. You are the God who creates and brings forth life and you are the life that is brought forth. How can you not want to take the time to know about you? Stop ignoring you and begin to understand you a little better. You are absolutely everything and everything is you.

*A*s you look within your own self you will begin to see your own patterns and you will begin to magnify what you must work on. This is to allow you to see these areas more clearly. As you magnify or intensify your pain you will begin to project it outward. What ultimately occurs is that you begin to see you in everyone else. Every time that you project your pain forward you are allowed to look at it and to release it. The only problem that you may run into in this process is the belief that it is not yours. You will find ways to convince yourself that your pain is not being projected outward and that what you are seeing or feeling is actually being projected to you from the other individual or individuals. In other words, you do not wish to own your pain so you convince yourself that it is someone else's stuff.

You usually project onto someone close and usually it is someone from whom you want something. You are usually relying on this person to meet your needs in some way. It may be a boss or associate at work. It may also be a relative or spouse. You primarily are seeking to meet your needs and, when you do not fulfill your needs to your satisfaction, you get your feelings hurt or you just get mad. And as you get more and more angry you project this outward also. You then begin to "believe" that he or she is the angry one or that he or she is the one who is trying to get their needs met. Whatever you are doing is what is being projected forward and reflected back to you. You create it all. If it is so big that it cannot be ignored then I highly suggest you own it and allow it to release. You need not point your finger at someone else when it is all your projected stuff that you are viewing.

Now; here is the interesting part. You may honestly believe that it is not your stuff. You may feel as though you have nothing to do with what you are seeing. I will repeat for you once again that "if it is not in you, you will never see it." If you do see it, it is coming from inside of you and you are now seeing it so that you might realize it is yours and, by doing so, release it. You are in a position now to release those things which are being magnified for you. You will see you in everyone. You will not see your neighbor or your mother or your father, you will see yourself. As you see yourself in others do not judge nor condemn them, as what you are seeing is really you and you will be condemning and judging you.

As you learn to move more freely within yourself you will be allowed to see more areas within you. Sometimes it will be a while before you explore certain areas, and, when you do, you will be surprised at what you find within you. You will see that everything you have ever noticed about another person is only noticed because it is part of you and it triggers your part and that is why it is noticed in the first place. Once you learn how everyone is only a mirror for you, you will stop blaming and judging your mirrors for how you look. You will begin to clean you out so that you might release your hold on whatever it is that displeases you. You will also learn to appreciate yourself by knowing that you are projecting parts of you outward to be reflected back to you. You will see in certain individuals (your mirrors) things that you love about you as well as things that you hate. You may find that you are as unconscious about the parts you love as you are about the parts you hate.

Once you wake up to self-discovery you will be waking up to the self and the self is God. As you learn to grow and to become more of you, you will seek out more of you in others (your mirrors). You will want to take a closer look and to see why you are judging some so harshly. Remember, in judging them you judge you, because what you see is coming from you in the form of a projection. You cannot see anything that you do not own within you. When you learn to consciously own it you will be taking responsibility for yourself as the creator of your world. If you continue to push your stuff off on others so that you might stay blind, you will only be creation and you will not become whole. You become whole by owning all parts of you. You are cause and effect. You are movement and stagnation. You are God as well as creation. Everything is God and God is everything. When you discover how you do this you will have discovered a very big piece of you. You create it all and you become it all.

As you learn to overcome some of your own beliefs in limitation and judgment, you will be allowed to move forward into a much grander view of yourself. Right now you are seeing yourself from a very limited perspective, and soon your sense of self will expand and your perspective will expand. For now, I want you to know that you are wasting time and energy by pointing out flaws in others. They are your flaws and the sooner you own them the sooner you become whole.

༺❀༻

As you begin to release your hold on who you now are, you will allow yourself the opportunity to become new. Have you ever wished you had a new life or that you could start all over? This is what you will be doing. You will be starting over with a new way of seeing everything and this will give you the chance to rethink and re-feel every choice you have ever made. You get to start fresh. You get to be born again in the light and you get to receive all the assistance you may not have received the first time. This is due to the fact that you are now using parts of you that were not available to you in your past. Now that more of you is becoming a part of you, you have more options and you have more to work with.

You have let go of a great deal in your belief system and this allows for more of you to enter and to use you as you were intended. You were never meant to stay unconscious. You were always meant to wake up at some point and to become all that you are currently becoming. A little knowledge goes a long way and you are wisdom "becoming." You are growing in wisdom by learning to see things from a new perspective. As you learn to let go of more and more of your old beliefs (old programming) you will be allowing yourself to expand in awareness. This expansion is what is stretching you and making you a little uncomfortable. This expansion is also what is causing you to shift-up. This is the whole idea. You move out of darkness on your own by shifting into light awareness, and you are automatically lifted up.

As you begin to see how you are achieving this rise up, you will wish to acknowledge how you are transforming you. You are changing and you were growing and you are learning how you are God. You are creating you as you go and you are allowing the part of you that is God to "be." You are allowing all parts of you to take on new roles and you are allowing you to be changed. You are creating new ways of viewing life and you are creating new ways of existing in life. You are seeing through new eyes, and you are beginning to know that you and God are one and the same. You are in the body of God and God is in you. You are one. As you begin to realize this you will begin to allow yourself to be your creator. You will not push away the idea that God works in you.

You now believe that God would not take on such a loathsome job because you see yourself as loathsome. This too shall change. You will begin to see how valuable each of you are and this will allow you to believe that God would reach into your life and "give to you." You will find that God does not loathe you and God does not think that you are not worth his efforts. God is not too busy for you despite what you may believe. God is very much concerned with what goes on within his body and you are part of that body. You and God are one. Why would God not care what happens to you? God cares. God is now in a position to let himself assist you only because you opened the door to let God in. Once you invite God in, you are in a position to be helped by God.

As you learn to connect with your own God self you will begin to feel extraordinary events take place within you and sometimes they will appear to be outside of you. You will find that dimensions cross and you can see into the past and you can see the future. You will be allowed to erase the barriers that stand between one reality and another. You will be allowed to form your own reality based on what you now believe. As you form this reality it will take on life. It will begin to pulse and to vibrate and it will take on a life of its own. Each time you shift your consciousness you will be shifting your reality. It will expand as you expand and it will grow as you grow. It is an entire world that was created by your perception and it is now alive and you are *in* it.

You become what you believe and if you believe in love and beauty you get to become love and beauty. If you believe in pain and injustice and ugliness your world will be one of pain, injustice and ugliness. You go forward in your world. It is a bubble around you. You live in what you have created. I simply want to show you how to transform your world (your bubble) from one of pain, injustice and ugliness to a world (bubble) of love and beauty with wisdom of God.

You will find that you no longer wish to create worlds of pain. You have created for so long from unconsciousness and now it is time to wake up and know that you create it all, and, since you create it all, you can change it all. What a wonderful gift to give you. You get to change it because you now have been given the information that says, "Well, it's all yours. Do with it what you will." Without that information you would continue to stumble around in the darkness and not know that you have the ability to turn on a light and see what you are doing. Now is the time. We are turning you on!

❧

When you become totally engrossed in your own healing process, you begin to take on a new sense of something much larger than you are. You begin to feel how others affect you and how you affect others. You will find that those who push your buttons are often the ones who are being affected by you most. They are having their buttons pushed by you and so you create conflict. If you do not wish to create conflict you may simply begin to resist the urge to tell them how wrong they are or to tell them how they "should be" (according to how you see it).

They too will have complaints about you and they too will wish to set you straight. You have met someone who sees differently than you do and I suggest you allow them to view reality any way they like. Your job is not to set them straight, as you do not know what straight is. You do not even know how you got to believe what you believe, so how can you tell someone else how it is or direct them in how they should behave? You are lost and the most you can do in your current state is direct others on how to be lost. You must learn to "give up" telling others how to act and how to live. You take care of you and allow God to take care of the rest of creation.

Now; when you begin to see how you intervene in other people's lives you will begin to see how you are focusing on them because you do not wish to focus on you. You are looking at their faults because you do not wish to give up your own. You turn what they do into something awful so that you do not have to be the one who is wrong. You will find that you are wrong to the extent that you believe you are right. You are also wrong to the degree that you believe that you are right. Whenever you believe yourself to be right and another to be wrong you are creating more wrong for yourself. You create everything in your world and you are the only one who lives in your world or your private belief system. If you make others wrong you are making wrong a part of your world. If you make wrong a part of your world you must then be part of your world which is now based on wrong.

Do not live in a world of right and wrong. Move into a world of simply accepting and being. Allow wrong-doing to become a thing of the past. Do not judge you and do not judge others. You judge you and do not realize how much you do. You will see how much you are judging you by making yourself "aware" of every situation in which you judge another. Judgment is based solely on a decision to make something not good. Stop making things not good. Allow everything to be good. Do not make people around you 'not' good. Allow everything they do to be good and for a purpose. You do not know what their purpose for lying or cheating or killing is, but it is for a purpose and it has nothing to do with evil. Give evil a rest and let evil leave your world, by no longer using it as a tagging system for every action that you cannot comprehend. God is in charge and God knows why things occur. Why not ask God before you begin to call someone wrong or ignorant? You do not know that you are God so how can you know that everyone else is God?

❧

As you begin to emerge as a butterfly you will be hesitant to try out your wings. You will not know how to fly except instinctually. As you learn more and more about your ability to take wing and fly, you will begin to see how you have been grounded for a great period of time and you never realized that you were. When you come to this realization you will begin to let go of your need to be in control. Your need for control is simply a part of your grounded-ness. Once you are flying, you will no longer feel it necessary to direct every little move in life. You will begin to feel as though you are being guided by the wind and you will begin to see how you are. As you begin to learn more about the dynamics of creation you will begin to see how creation is here to assist you. You are actually a part of creation and all parts of you are able to assist you as you rise. You need only connect with and begin to use these various parts of you.

As you begin to leave behind the more destructive parts, you will find yourself more creative and less destructive. You will find yourself receiving as you have never before received. You will also find yourself being one with everyone and with life. You will begin to relate to others on an entirely new level. You will begin to see how you are good and to let go of your belief that part of you is bad. As you grow more and more into receiving, you will begin to show your own self how you do deserve and how you are good to you. As you show you how good you are, you will begin to allow for the goodness of life. You are now in a position to be practically whatever you can imagine. You are beginning to create for yourself from love of self. As this process continues you will begin to feel as though you are in love and you will be in love, or in the light. When you begin to live in the light you will find that you have unlimited resources and you have no one to put you down because "you" are no longer putting you down.

As you grow in this experience you will begin to see how you are also growing within and it is being reflected out into your world. You are one of the light beings who are being born. You are literally being born of light and it is all by your choice to do so. As you learn to accept your light you will learn that expansion is the way to go. Grow in light and you grow in God. Grow in light and you grow in love. You are the light of the world and you have the ability to create love in your world. Perception is all in how you view any given situation or event. You may create your perception so that you see everything from love or you may create it so that you see everything from fear. Love and fear are your choices at any given moment and in any given situation. You may learn to release enough self-doubt to always come from love. You shut the door on love when you doubt. You open the door for love when you trust. You are now learning to trust and to "let go" of doubt. It is time to move forward and it is time to move into love

☙❧

Once you begin to feel the shift, both in consciousness and in your physical body, you will begin to see how your body is connected to your mind. When you hurt your body your mind is affected. When you hurt your mind your body is affected. Please do not hurt yourself and you will not need pain. Pain is a result of not needing joy. If you are in pain you have let go of joy and you have decided that pain suits you best. When you learn that you deserve joy you will let go of your need to draw pain of any kind. Most of you have strong religious beliefs which stop you from too much joy. You do not want to get results from carnal pleasures as it would lead to sin. Sin is very big in religion and so you deprive yourself of joy in certain areas in order to comply to your religious beliefs. Those of you who have no religion are still trapped in the morality cycle that has been established here on this plane. "No sex" is probably your biggest try at stopping pleasure. Some of you even have the ability to turn pleasure into pain by simply stopping or blocking the movement of energy.

As you begin to uncover more of your pattern you will begin to see how you not only do not wish to continue with your current pattern, you also do not wish to break your current pattern. You might say that you are stuck. You don't want to continue on the way you have and yet you don't want to change. So; what can one do when one has become aware of the fact that one is changing, and yet part of one does not wish to surrender to change? Be very patient with yourself. You will begin to see how you may be able to move into change in a very gentle fashion if you are patient.

Most of what you are dealing with has to do with shame. Sin has invented shame. Without sin there would be no shame. Just think, no wrong ever - no way to create shame. What a lovely place you would be in if you gave up shame. You shame one another in order to control one another. Now it is time to let go of the shame that stops you from believing that you are innocent. You have created no sins and you do no wrong. You are simply God expressing in matter and I really don't think that could be sinful in any way. You are creative energy rising and falling like the tide. How could that be a sinful act? You create as you go and you do not require shame to stop you. Shame will take you out of your joy very quickly and you will find that you are not only 'not' a sinner you are also not evil and full of bad. You are good, and someone who is good does not require shame.

As you begin to clear your shame I wish you to be very good to your "self" and to love your "self." Do not get caught up in the need to expose your "self" or to put your "self" down. You are clearing your shame in order to set you free of sin. If you let go of sin you will find innocence once again. With innocence comes the freedom you require to heal completely. As you heal completely you will become complete and whole. Your wholeness has to do with your lack of separation and your ability to touch and to love all parts of you.

You have been taught that parts of you are not holy. That is a lie. You are a holy being and you are God expressing in matter. There is no wrong way and there is no right way. When you let go of that, you will learn to accept the "self" which is your divine "self." You are the divine and you are so confused that you call you evil. You may not think that you do, but watch how much criticism you have for those around you and you will know how much criticism you have for your own "self." You are light and you are dimming your "self" by calling you dark. Let go of sin. It does not exist.

⚜

You will begin to see how you have created not only your own defense mechanisms; you have also created your own hazards. You begin by telling yourself that you will not do this or that, and that you do not wish to be hurt so you will not allow this or that to occur. As you build up more and more resistance to this or that, you will be seeing "this or that" as more and more dangerous. This is how you make mountains out of mole hills. You literally create any given situation into a personal danger by running from it all your life.

As you learn to face your fears you will want to face your emotional dangers. It will become wise to get over your fear of rejection and your fear of abandonment by going right into these fears. You all experience them to one degree or another. Most of you are so afraid of being abandoned that you would feel lost without the one you have chosen to play the role of your mate. The rest of you who have no mate are dealing with rejection and abandonment also. It became so built up and so dangerous that you decided "not to get involved" in a relationship. Your danger factor is just too big. You cannot break through your fears to even begin a relationship with a mate. So; whether you sit alone or are with a mate, you still carry these fears.

As you begin to break through the barriers that you have created for yourself you will begin to feel a sense of freedom. You will feel that you have broken through some barrier and you will have. You will also begin to feel as though you are strong. The greater you become the greater you feel. You will feel as though you could take on the world and it will be because you are taking on your own world. You will be shifting and shaping and changing your own self which is the core of your own world. All of your rules are either created by you or adopted by you. You may decide to keep a few or you may throw all of the rules right out the window and into the universal catch-all.

As you learn to let go of rules that protect you from rejection and from abandonment, you will begin to let go of your fear of your mate or your friends. You see, you transfer your fear of losing onto others and they become the focus of your fear. You begin by seeing them as someone you need for security or friendship or lack of loneliness. As you grow more and more attached you begin to project an image onto them. They may not be at all what you are seeing them as, because it is your projection. You want someone to be a certain way so that you can feel safe and loved and accepted. When they start being themselves and breaking the mold or projection that you have created for them, you get upset. They are not what you projected. They are not following the rules - your rules - for staying safe. They are doing their own thing and this becomes upsetting for you.

You live by your rules because it feels safe. "Your rules" may make someone else feel very unsafe and even uncomfortable. You must let go of "your need" to project "your rules" for safety onto another. It is time to love unconditionally and to set yourself free of fear of abandonment and fear of rejection. You will all move into the flow when you give up the need for protection and let go of the need for projection. Keep your rules to yourself and allow them to be transformed.

꧁꧂

*A*s you begin to see how you are being exposed to your own awareness you will begin to feel the difference between blindness and seeing. You will begin to feel how delightful it can be to see your patterns after so many years of not seeing. It will also be good for you to know you and understand you a little better. Most of what you wish to believe has little to do with what is true and a great deal to do with how you were taught to comprehend any given situation. Many of you are self-taught and you began by learning in childhood how to figure things out for yourself. If you were neglected or abused you may think a little different than most. You may have what I will call lopsided thinking and you may have brought this lopsided thinking forward in your adult life.

As you look at how you think and feel about any given situation I wish you to open to a new way of seeing everything. A hurt child will think defensively and react defensively. This is due to the fact that he or she does not know how to act openly. If you are injured or shut up or hit in any way, you begin to protect yourself. Now you are an adult and you are still protecting yourself and your methods are no longer viable. You must learn to let go of protection and to open to life. I know this frightens you but it is how you will learn to raise yourself up out of fear.

As you begin to release your defenses you will be releasing a great store of energy. This energy is put in place to protect and defend. It takes a lot of energy to constantly "watch out for" evil and hurt. If you can learn to trust God you will be safe in letting go of your defenses. As you let go of your defenses you will begin to see and feel the freedom of letting go. You literally relax and let go. It will feel very good and you will enjoy the flow of letting go. When you first begin to show yourself how this works you may frighten yourself and wish to put your defensive wall of protection back up. But if you are going to be free you must come out of hiding and face the world as well as yourself.

If you have built big walls to protect yourself you may find them crumbling and you may find your world changing drastically. If you have let go to the extent that you have reached the core of your pain, you will be confused about your own action or inaction in any given situation. You will no longer be playing by the rules that you once set in place for yourself and this may be confusing for you. You see, you are accustomed to following these rules even though the danger is long past. You may have developed a set of rules to protect you or you may have developed a set of rules to assist you in forgetting your painful experiences. Either way, you are locked in by your rules and now it is time to break your own rules.

As you begin to go into your deepest desires and wants and needs you will begin to see how your rules for defense block energy. Your rules for defense were once made to keep you safe from harm and now they are outdated and hang around your neck like a noose. You will find that when you can break free of your rules you will feel much lighter. You need not stay locked into those outdated modes of protection. Some of you withdraw and hide while others attack and provoke. Whatever your defensive position is I wish you to begin to release it.

You are so protected that you fight off anyone who comes too close to you. You must learn to accept and to be free of limitation. Stop arguing for it is you defending you. You need not defend for you are no longer going to attack you. Your greatest enemy is the voice you use to judge you and criticize you. You put up such a defensive attitude with others because you are so tired of being criticized and you are the one criticizing you. Give you a break and allow yourself to knock down all the walls by giving up the need for self-denial and self-punishment. This is going to be a very big step for you, and it will feel very good once you can learn to praise you instead of criticize you.

As you realize how you have used your own voice to parent you and continue screaming at you, you will find that you are the one who creates all the misery and all the hard feelings in your own life. As you learn to see how this works you will be very happy to let go. If you wish to see how much or how often you criticize you, you may do so by listening to how much or how often you criticize the world around you. When you stop judging and criticizing others you will have let go of your own self-criticism. Others are simply volunteer reflections and they are only showing you who you are and what you do.

※

*A*s you begin to come into yourself you will begin to "feel" more. You will feel as though you are more sensitive and you will feel as though you are beginning to change. The most wonderful part of being born again into your own body is that you may change what you do not like. At some point in your development you will even begin to change the molecular structure of your own body. As you learn to become stronger in your healing ability you will be using more parts of you to attain all that you desire on the material level. As you use more parts of you, you begin to strengthen these parts simply by their usage. You will discover that the majority of "you" is not in use. In the same way that you only use approximately five percent of your brain power, you also only use approximately five percent of you. Think of how much of you is missing! This is a time for making you whole and bringing all of you into you.

You are being born into matter. God is coming into you. You are the pod or the embryo that "receives" all that is light. Do not shut down or shut out any part of you. If you have anger - own it. If you have low self-esteem - own it. If you are rude and obnoxious - own it. If you are joyful and happy - own it, and if you wish to die - own it. Do not be afraid to own any and all parts of you for it will allow you to become whole. If you give up trying to be good little girls and boys you will do better at allowing all parts of you to coexist. It will help if you begin to accept what you call the bad parts in you. You will know what you label as bad in you by looking at what you label as bad in others. Once you have made a list of all that you despise in others you will know what you are despising in your own self. As you learn to allow these parts to coexist with the rest of you, you will be gaining more of you and you will come into balance. Remember - to love is to accept!

As you begin to accept more and more parts of you, you will be allowing the dark to turn to light. You will be choosing love (acceptance) over fear and you will be creating harmony within your own beingness. As you continue to grow and to learn and to develop, you will see changes occur more easily and more readily within you. You will no longer be struggling to hold-on to your old way of being, for you will have realized the beauty in changing you and healing you. Whenever you feel the urge to change how another behaves it is "your urge" to change. Keep it at home and work on you. Give up working on others until you have ascended to a new level of awareness within your own beingness. You will know when you have arrived at a new level of beingness, for you will no longer push at the world to change. You will be one with God and you will know that to change, one must only concentrate on the self and all else falls in step. You are the leader. You are becoming one with God.

❧

As we begin to ascend we begin to feel a little light-headed and maybe even nauseous. This is due in part to the speed at which you will be vibrating. You will have speeded up your reproduction of cellular memory as well as your reproductive skills. Your cells will be vibrating and your whole body will be raising its consciousness to a new height. This will be the first part of your ascension. Your rise up out of third dimensional reality will be quite a step for you. You will begin to accept parts of you that have been stifled and you will begin to see all life from a brand new perspective. For the first time you will continue to grow instead of contracting into death. You will continue your expansion of the self within the self and you will continue to expand God consciousness. As you begin the speed up of vibration your body will need to adjust. You will wish to be patient with your body as you go through the various steps necessary to allow you to change or shift into new consciousness.

The universe is assisting in this process and all parts of life are being affected. The more you "feel" the greater the impact will be on your body and your psyche. As you begin to rise up in consciousness you will begin to feel how you are changing and how your body is literally growing through this change as well. You will find that the body has various ways to rid itself of toxic waste and toxic behavior. Do not get upset when you begin to clear debris through your pores or your mouth or your eyes. You will also clear through your male and female genitals as well as the kidneys and colon. Your body will rid through whatever means possible and a variety of symptoms may occur. Do not worry. You are physical as well as spiritual and you are taking your body into the fourth dimension with you. You are spiraling up and taking your body as you go.

As you begin to require less and less thoughtfulness and more awareness, you will begin to see how you are no longer a logical being. You are moving beyond logic and into awareness. Awareness is made of knowingness combined with information that is whole. It is not a product of your imagination as is wisdom. Wisdom is the use of imagination to combine what you do not know and learn more. You will find that knowledge and the ability to learn are connected. Sometimes you have too much knowledge and you think you have all the answers, so you will not receive wisdom. Wisdom is all imagination combined with all information. When you combine imagination and information you may then make it into all types of new realities. You need not be stuck in non imaginative realities. You might as well learn to enjoy your creative ability and begin to create from pure imagination. Make it up as you go.

Do not be afraid to change how you think and do not be afraid to break out of your mold. You are like a chick who is breaking out of its egg. You are hatching and becoming alive. You are going to grow into the wisdom and wonder of God as the wisdom and wonder of God grows in you. You are now in transition and your body will begin to feel it. You have read enough and experienced enough to create a great shift in consciousness. I believe you are aware of the power of the written word and I believe you also fear written words. You will learn that all power is yours and what you are really afraid of is you. You will learn to accept you and you will learn to love you instead of fear you. You are God "becoming."

As you grow into a whole being you will be becoming all that you were meant to be. Most of you come to earth and never germinate into your totality. You always stop short and develop rules to follow instead of developing new ways to view reality. As you become unstuck you will begin to know freedom and a powerful creative ability. It is your ability to create and it is your ability to see whatever you choose to see. At this instant you may choose to see something as bad or wrong or you may choose to see that very same thing as good or right. As you choose, you literally decide how you will view "your" reality. You choose on a daily basis whether your life is good or bad by how you view everything that occurs in it. As you learn to take off your distorted glasses and view everything as perfect, you will begin to see only perfection.

Once you become all that you can be you will also expand into your life. Your life will become more loving and more peace-filled as you become loving and peace-filled. You will find that your only purpose is love and your only reason to seek out love is your distorted view of reality. As we bring you back into focus and allow you to be who you are you will begin to see that you are not only no longer fear, you are not even evil. You have decided to switch views and see yourself as good and this will create giant shifts in your daily life. Most of what you have begun to view as good is what makes you feel good. This too is simply perception and will change as you go.

Most of your description of good has to do with "feel good" things. Things which make you feel good are not always a good idea. Sometimes you have cause and effect working against you. For example: you do not wish to stop breathing and yet you smoke and inhale poison directly into your lungs; or you put yourself on a drug that will later toxify and poison your system. These are just two extreme versions of something that "feels good" but is best to avoid doing to your "self." If you love your "self" you will want to care for your "self." You are your parent now. How do you rate as a parent? Do you love you? Are you good to you? Do you "care" if you are well or sick? If you have those who don't seem to care about you I suggest you look at how you do not care about you. You are learning to love and nurture your "self." Please stop poisoning your "self." You are God!

❦

*A*s you begin the breakdown of cellular memory, you will begin to observe your own world from a whole new perspective. As you begin to lose the programming that has kept you set in one direction, you may find yourself spinning in many directions or simply not moving at all. This is part of letting go of your neuro-linguistic programming. It is a part of you that copies, or reacts to, certain stimulus in a specific manner.

As you begin to release this type of programming you will be letting go of a very big part of you. You have spent a great deal of time putting yourself through hell because you believe you are stupid. Most of you do not even know that you believe you are stupid, but you still do. You question your motives and you question your credibility. You can tell how much you question your own stupidity by watching how often you criticize others for being stupid or for not making sensible choices. You decide what is dumb or ugly or stupid and then you want everyone else to live by your judgment of any given event. When you learn to let go of these rules you will never see another as stupid, which means that you will have let go of seeing yourself as stupid.

When you learn to let go of competition and to simply "do your own thing," no matter how abnormal "your own thing" appears, you will have learned to harness your own quality and drive. You have created your own world filled with your creative ideas. You need never compete for anything. You need never judge anyone as less than another. You need never be afraid to be who you are.

You are God creating for God and if you follow the rules set out for competition you will continue to create a bigger problem than already exists in your world. You are working yourselves to death when you could be relaxing. You make all of your choices about how you will live and most of the time you are striving to "do better" and "have more" and "look good" to the world. Stop striving. Begin to accept where you are. Allow yourself to have less in the way of opulence and more in the way of peace, contentment and relaxation. Someone taught you to struggle and to spend all your money to look better or to keep up with the neighbors. It is not necessary to compete. It is only necessary to love. You may let go of your finery because if you do not it is going to bury you. You have lost control and your "stuff" controls you. You cannot move because it costs too much to move all your stuff. Some of you even put your "stuff" in storage and pay someone else to hold on to it for you.

You are losing touch with your spiritual needs by surrendering to competition. You cannot think about what you need spiritually because you are so busy "keeping up" with what you believe is a good way to live. Who says so? How did you get so programmed to the idea that to give up all your time to make money is a good idea. Balance is a good idea. Let's try to balance our time so that you give time to you. If your time is worth money to someone else can you imagine how much it is worth to you?

❧

*A*s you begin to see how you operate, you will begin to change your mode of operation. This will be out of an understanding of your own inner workings. You are being reprogrammed and it is about time. You have carried your cellular memory and your feelings of hurt and danger for long enough. Now you are transforming these hurt feelings into something that is helpful instead of harmful. You will no longer pretend to be how you wish to be viewed. You will now *become* all that you are and you will be allowed to drop the pretense. You all act and pretend. From childhood you were taught to not feel. If you hurt and you began to cry you were told to be quiet or you were given something to take your mind off of your hurt. Now, when you hurt, you either distract yourself by overworking, or overeating, or overplaying, or you punish yourself if you cry out in pain.

To cry out is your only way to express your pain and yet it is unacceptable for you to cry. Did you ever cry as a child and have an adult role model say, "Yes, that's good. Get it all out?" No, I don't think you did. You all want to stop pain and to shut it off at any cost. You are in pain now and to learn to cry would assist you in releasing any pent-up feelings of rage and frustration. You must learn to release trapped energy in constructive ways so you will not act-out your rage and, by doing so, cause someone else to pick up on your rage and continue your cycle of feelings. If you can, try to cry and scream and hit (pillows) and unblock the feelings that are trapped in you. If you fail at first do not worry. Your emotions will break down and begin to release at some point. They cannot "hold on" to you forever.

You have begun to touch you in places you never knew you existed. This is due in part to your ability to go within and work out your energy blocks, and it is a direct result of desire. The desire to heal creates healing and you get to see where you have been sick. The desire to heal also brings forward the need to love and be loved. As you learn to love your own self you will be moving energy in great volumes. This energy is you and it has laid dormant in you. This is love and it is light and it has healing properties.

Once you release your trapped and blocked feelings you will be allowed to use all parts of you without depending on rules and judgments. Most of what you will be doing is uncovering layers of old outdated thoughts. These are thoughts that got trapped and were never used again on a conscious level. This does not mean that these thoughts have been inactive. They have been working in you for years and even for lifetimes. These thoughts often control you. You have lost the ability to know who you are because you have been run in so many directions by dead or no longer valid thoughts. These thoughts are energy and they have power. All energy has power. This is what you are being stripped of. You are losing your power and turning your power over to God. God says you are good and wonderful and everything that occurs is for a reason. What do you say? How do you "feel" about you? Are you in love with you or do you hate you?

You will begin to enter a phase in your healing where you uncover the parts of you who do not like you. You will find that, not only do you not like things about yourself; you also have parts of you who do not like you back. This will be a messy area to heal. Be ready for what you would call bad feelings and low self-worth. After all, how can you hold on to high self-worth when you are uncovering the parts of you who do not like you? You will find that the more you uncover the more you will eventually grow in love and in light. In the beginning, however, you will deal with some very bad feelings that are directed towards you by you. I know you never meant to hate you but you did accomplish just that. Now we will un-layer your self-hate and learn to release it and allow you to be who you are. No more rules to say how guilty you are or how worthless and stupid you are. You will learn to be whole and with wholeness comes wellness and peace.

When you are well, you will no longer feel uncomfortable living in you. You will no longer hate parts of you and those parts will take their cue from you and they will start to accept you. This is the battle within. Darkness (confusion, ignorance) is fighting with the light. Darkness fears the light. The light is acceptance and love. How can confusion and ignorance survive in the face of acceptance and love? Something has got to give. Part of you must surrender to a greater part of you. Do you feel confused and upset? Do not worry it will all work itself out. God is in you. How did God get in you? You asked. Don't you remember? You invited God in. God does not go uninvited so you are now hosting God. You are the one who creates everything in your life. You created your fall and now you are creating your rise up out of the fall. You did not always live so unconscious as you now do, you know? This was just a sleep time, an incubation period. It's time to begin the waking process now. Are you ready? Can you feel it coming?

❧

Whenever you begin to raise your level of consciousness you will have a direct opposite pull. You will want to be pulled right back down into your old position or belief structure. This is due, in part, to the fact that you had been stuck in that position for so long. You will want to think of it much as you would a tooth that has been straightened by braces. Once you straighten out the tooth you must wear a retaining gear to keep it from falling back into its old crooked hole. You must wait until the old hole grows over then the straightened tooth will be embedded in a new foundation. You will find that once you rise to a new position of intelligence through awareness, you will be pulled back into your old behaviors periodically, and you will fluctuate back and forth until you can get a good foothold in your new higher position up the ladder of consciousness.

As you begin to prepare for your ascent you must remember that you are fragile and you have lain in darkness for eternity. It will only be natural that you fluctuate until you become enough light to keep you out of the dark. As you become more adept at staying "up" you will begin to look around you and see your new perspective. You will begin to flow more easily with what occurs around you and you will begin to see the benefits in being patient. You are learning to raise your own energy to new heights and to do so requires that you take all parts of you with you. You are learning to accept all parts of you so that you might go up. As you go up you become lighter and life becomes lighter.

There are no heavy burdens once you lighten up! You will find that everything that brings you down is you. You will find that others do not and cannot bring you down. You only give in to others and accept their put-downs. You never get in a bad mood because of what someone does or says. You only get in a bad mood because you accept what is being said as the truth. If someone infers that you are stupid it does not disturb you unless you already have programming in you that tells you "I am stupid." If you have this programming it will cause you to be upset. What is upsetting to you is not that another put you down by saying "you are stupid" but the fact that you "believe" yourself to be stupid. Someone just confirmed what you believe, so I suggest you become grateful for the chance to find out what you carry instead of getting angry at the messenger. The one who shows you yourself is only doing a service that you requested.

Now; what you would be best off doing in this case would be to reassert your teacher self and begin to reprogram the "I am stupid" into "I am smart." This can be done with affirmations written daily or by repeating constantly and on a daily basis "I am smart."

When you begin to see how powerful it can be to reprogram yourself, you will wish to let go of your old beliefs and adopt all new ones. Any time you feel bad about the attitude of another person towards yourself, look at what it represents and then change the belief inside of you. You will find that reprogramming takes a little time but is well worth the effort. I want to leave you with this thought. You are what you believe and you will become what you believe. Believe what you want!

*A*s you learn how to detect and to allow your impulsiveness to subside, you will find that you no longer need to act on every impulse. Sometimes an impulse is simply a spring that has sprung and sometimes an impulse is your own behavior gone crazy. You will find that you may move impulsively or act impulsively and still be okay. Not all impulsiveness is a burden. Sometimes the signal that runs from your brain to your body does so, so quickly that you feel compelled to do what is being requested without taking the time to think. This is, of course, impulsive and yet it may also be a natural response. It may be that your brain is set in fifth gear and wants to move things along quickly, or it may be that what you are moving into frightens you and so you require extra thrust to go ahead with it. Impulsiveness is not necessarily a bad thing. Not everyone needs a lot of time to be moved into new situations.

It is often said that you should not be impulsive in your decisions and choices and yet your own body knows what it is doing when it signals you in such a fashion. You are learning to listen to your body and inner workings. This is a good place to start. You begin to feel an impulse to do something or to be somewhere for a reason. You also have impulses which tell you to stay or to go. You often silence your impulsiveness because you have been taught to be more rational and to think everything through. If you have an impulse to act on something, you may not move until it is too late and you may not connect with the energy that is being sent in your direction. As you learn how you are organic and hooked-up to all nature, you will begin to see the benefit of looking at impulses as a signal from the part of you who is connected to your instincts and nature.

As you learn to uncover more of your natural instincts and knowledge, you will begin to feel more comfortable within your own body. There will no longer be such a struggle within the will to impose its way on the totality of you. You are more than a will and you will respond to more than your own will power. As you learn to handle energy from a new level of operation within yourself, you will begin to see how all energy is connected and can be used anywhere you wish. You may even find that you have been using energy to deplete yourself instead of enhance yourself. As you learn to operate within the realms of trust and faith you will find that you no longer know who you now are, as this you is only made up of rules and regulations set up by someone else. When you begin to accept you and trust you, you will be amazed at who and what you really are. You will be stupefied at the aggressiveness of yourself. You will begin to see your "self" evolving and growing.

As the "self" grows and evolves it will become more and it will learn more from within itself, and it will expand and you will have more of you instead of more programmed babble. You will be real instead of a package of results and regulations and beliefs. You will be a functioning pulsating organism and you will finally be plugged-in and tuned-in and turned-on. You will vibrate of your own accord and you will be a pulsating, vibrating spark of life itself. You will be reconnected with you and with your light. Your spark is your light. The spark is what keeps you going and ready to light up. The spark of light that is in you is for you to use. It is God consciousness and you may ignore it or use it. How do you use God? First you must accept that God is in you and allow God to be all that God is. It is not difficult, but you are so buried under your thinking and your belief system that it is tough to get you to drop the walls and barriers you have put up to keep you safe. It is your fear of God that keeps you from God. It is your fear of being God that keeps you from being God.

⚜

As you allow your inner sensory mechanics to learn to develop, you will find that you have an entirely new mechanism to work with. You will find that you have parts of you who do not know how to assist you. These newly uncovered parts will find it difficult to survive at first. You will want to shut them up or shut them down until you gain acceptance of them and begin to see their value. All parts of you serve a purpose and all parts of you belong with you to make you complete. As soon as you can learn to accept all parts, you will be held in a very precarious position within your own self. You will not be in you completely. You have the ability to walk around only half there. You also have the ability to walk around less than half there.

As you develop these other parts of you, you will find that time is actually your friend and not your foe. You will learn that it takes time to heal and it takes time to balance. The more time you can devote to your own self the faster you move along in this process. If you wish to move faster, simply be more aware of what you do and think and say. Do not focus on others, but instead, focus on you. You are the entire living organism that creates all that you see and experience. There is nothing to learn outside that you cannot learn doubly quick inside. You are all parts that you project. You are the projector and everything else is the screen. You are also the film that runs through the projector. The film is creation and how you view it. The film is life process and it is also the twists and turns of your own mind. You project out scenes which will please you and scenes which will upset you. You allow love and you allow fear. You do this in order to be released from what you have created. If you created it you can un-create it. If you called it awful and horrible you can call it something else. It is all your creation.

Once you learn how various parts of you create and then project out what is created, you will learn how to create projections that are more conducive to love, joy and peace. Right now you have too many parts of you fighting against love, joy and peace. We don't want boredom so peace is out. We don't want to accept everything we see so love is out. And we don't want to let things go unpunished so joy is out. Ah! But you shall change and let go of your need for justice and stimulation and rejection. When you change you will see love, joy and peace on a daily basis, with no interference from struggle between what you really want and what you have been taught to want. You are love as well as rejection of love, and soon the love will overcome the rejection and fear. Love will be bigger in time. Give yourself time. It is a very big gift.

༄ྃ

As you begin to function in a new realm, you will begin to see changes in the way that your body responds to the environment. Most of you do not realize how organic you are. If you did, you would no longer put all the chemicals in you and you would not misuse your body in order to satisfy your ego. As you learn how to manifest in the realm of creation, you will be learning to accept you as a living, breathing organism. As you begin to see yourself as an organism you will stop punishing you for living and going in the wrong direction. After all, you don't punish your plants do you? If a plant sprouts out in one direction and you wanted it to grow straight you do not reject it or punish it. You simply work with it to train it to grow straight. Well, I want you to start working with you. Stop punishing you with your put-downs and criticism. You are pushing you down and you will never grow if you are pushed back down.

When you have learned how to love and nurture yourself you will begin to flower like a beautiful plant. The glory and wonder of your own organic beingness will begin to show. You will expand and explode with beauty. You will leave behind the anger and rage that has been your security blanket for so long. How will you survive without anger? It will be difficult at first. You are so attached to your cold cynicism and your burning rages. If you could not heat-up in an argument how could you energize? If you could not ridicule how could you feel superior? If you could not turn cold and leave, how could you prove you are better than? And if you cannot turn your back and exit dramatically, how can you show that you have courage and determination enough to walk out on everything? You will soon learn that to live without anger and rage is not an easy thing to do. You are very into acting out your dramas and giving your opponents a very good run for their money.

You all "act-out." Every one of you has your drama or your game that you play. Learn to recognize what you are doing and you will be able to call yourself on your own game. When you expose your game it will then end. It will be exposed for what it is and that will take all the fun out of it. As you learn to detect your games you will also see how you set the game up just to give you a thrill. No, you don't do this consciously but you do it just the same.

As you learn to break out of your games you will be learning to let go of your own programmed experiences. As you grew up you began to use your childhood games in new ways. You catch someone just as you did in childhood. If the game was set up in such a way as to manifest a single assailant or victim you will use this process in some area of your adult life. Maybe you only find one person who does not fit in and who must be exposed for being wrong. If you played where many victims were portrayed you may find many victims in your adult life drama. Whatever games you set up in childhood you are still playing. If you add this to your real life drama and any abuse which may have been played out, you have a very complicated game. If your favorite game was "hide and seek" you have a great deal of experience hiding parts of you so they won't get caught and exposed. Everything is taught and everything can be exposed for what it is and re-taught in a new way.

When you finally learn how you are just growing and evolving and how nothing that you do is evil or bad, you will see how you are part of the much larger picture. You are the part that is missing and now you are becoming whole. Anyone who is not complete, in that they are denying parts of their beingness, is being given an opportunity to heal and to bring those parts to the light. All are going to the light. To go to the light is as simple as letting go of condemning and judging. When you go to the light you do not have to move, you only have to see it through light and allow it to be. All parts of you are light and when you can accept all parts as light you will no longer require walls to hide the dark parts behind. You started to call part of you bad and now you find places to hide that part. It is a lie. There are no bad parts of anyone. No one need hide in order to be accepted. You are God and God accepts all parts of God.

❧

*W*hen you begin to rebalance, you will be thrown off-balance at first. Your balance is always dependent on how you see life and how you view your reality. Now your reality is changing and so is your view or perception. As these things change it is only natural that your balance should change also. Don't look at it as though you are becoming off-balance. Look at it more as though you have always been off-balance and now you are shifting so you will feel balanced. "Balanced" is feeling all parts of you. You will feel parts that you have never before experienced. Sometimes you have experienced certain parts, but you believe you put them to sleep long ago. Not all parts will feel good to you. Some of your own feelings are so painful to you that you will want to run from them and to shut them off. It is best to accept them and to express them to your "self." Do not express them to others as they can only give you their interpretation of your feelings.

As these feelings begin to separate and grow, they will feel more powerful than they really are. This is due to the fact that they are your secret hidden part of you. These feelings are the ones you hide out of shame. They may include feelings of rage, anger, jealousy, envy, hatred, boorishness and even revenge. As you work your way through such feelings I wish you to own them and accept them and allow them to express to you. You have stifled them long enough and now it is time to release and own them. They are you! You are releasing a part of you and it will be difficult for you to own that which you have pushed away for so long. You may even begin to feel that there is something very wrong with you to have such feelings. You are growing into you and these feelings are an *acceptable* part of you. Once you can accept your own feelings without judging them as awful, you will be capable of accepting you. You will be able to love you! You will have achieved healing and health.

The ability to love the self is not an easy thing to attain. The ability to love and accept you as you are, will lead to the ability to receive and accept new levels of evolution on the part of your parts. You might say that you are growing into yourself and, as you do so, you create more of yourself. You are actually becoming more of you by releasing your hold on "hiding" all parts of you. If your emotions are strong when you release them it is only because you have *held them in* for so long. Now is a good time to remind you that all unhealed places must come to the surface in order to create perfect balance. The truth must come out and the lies will be exposed. Part of the truth is that you have never known all of you. You are constantly being told to "keep it quiet" and under control. What would have helped is to have you express it freely to yourself without the acting out process. If you could see and accept strong feelings that you have been told are negative to your well-being, you would be more aware of what you hold in you and how out of balance you are.

Now; when you begin to bring these out-of-balance feelings to the surface, you may truly feel that you are out-of-balance and going "off the deep end." You are not! You are healing and coming into balance. Some of your feelings have been so stifled that just to *feel* will be intimidating and make you uncertain if you are going insane. Remember; it is all God! It is all good. You are so afraid of insanity as it is strongly feared by everyone. You need not disturb the others with your new revelation on this, but it is best to allow a little insanity into your life. You have pushed away insanity for so long that you are truly limited in what you *believe* to be sane behavior. It is all a matter of *who says so*. Is it sane to hide and stifle parts of you so you will not look out of step or stand out? No, I do not think so. The sane thing to do is to reach into you and bring the energy forward. I know that many of you are doing this now and feeling quite uncomfortable with what you are bringing forward. This is a healing time and the trend is toward wholeness. Welcome to the world of wholeness! It becomes you....

❧

You will begin to see a major shift in the belief system of your world when you have changed enough. It will be the kind of shift that allows you to be whomever you wish with no room for judgment or criticism. The biggest problem you have now is the lack of trust and faith. It is very difficult to love yourself when you are constantly comparing yourself to others in order to meet higher standards. If you only knew how you look spiritually you would be able to let go of your physical perception of how you should be. You are moving towards the spiritual self and it is a difficult thing for you. This spirit is not consumed so much with where you are as it is with how you are. You are seen as a spiral that is rising up and it does not matter if you are rising in conjunction with others or if you are rising alone. The spirit does not care for competition and it does not play competitive games. Spirit is pure essence and will assist you in rising up because spirit knows you are meant to rise.

I will tell you now that you do not look for outer images in order to see if you are more or less than another. You do not grade, evaluate, nor judge. You do not pretend that you know more than your neighbor or mate and you do not raise your ego up to lead you. You will find that most of you have found a way to make you feel better. This way is by "finding fault." You feel safer if you can find fault with others and, in doing so, make yourself look better. You need not even verbalize these faults that you find. It is simply a game that you play to keep you safe. You feel better if you think others are not as smart or as beautiful or as good as you are. This is how you allow yourself to be okay - if they are so bad, you must be good. You will find that this type of competition is what hides part of you from you.

You are not the one to judge another as being a certain "type" of person. You can only see in another what you are, and you are categorizing and fragmenting you by judging or labeling them. Some of you do this verbally and others do this mentally. Either way, it does not show love for your "self." You are meant to love you, not to put you down and not to put others down so you might feel safe. If you can learn to be nonjudgmental you will come closer to trust and faith. Non-judgment consists of knowing that everyone and everything and every deed and every expression is God. Do not judge any part of God. Do not find it necessary to call something bad or good. Allow everything to be and you will find yourself in a very interesting position. You will be allowed to be and you will be allowed to expand. This will be due to the fact that you will unlimit yourself by taking off the chains of judgment that you are using to bind you and to keep others down also.

You will find that as you move into the part of you that is trust and faith you will be less afraid and more in love. You will be moving into love and compassion and you will leave your need to criticize you, simply because "when you leave mistrust you enter trust." It is so simple. If you want to feel better about God, about life, about you, show a little trust. Stop trying to know everything in order to control everything. You will find that trust will bring you closer to God and closer to your true essence. Trust is something that is no longer in use and I wish to bring it back. Trust has been pushed out in favor of control. Control says, "I am going to fix this and make it work."

God says, "I will handle everything if you will just trust that I will." You need not see immediate results if you have trust. You will find that you are more easily guided if you have trust. Allow trust to come in and you will feel safe. You will no longer feel the need to compete in order to feel special or to fit in.

You are now moving in a direction that will take you into trust and faith. Do not fight it. Allow it to be your new way of living. You are so tired of mistrusting and feeling unsafe. Let God wrap his big arms around you and guide you back to love. I'm sure you have heard the saying "a little trust goes a long way." It is true. Trust will heal you more quickly than any other tonic you might try. Trust is your way back home and into godliness. Trust is the answer to so many questions and trust is the one feeling you do not know. You will learn to accept trust and it will be a very big stretch for you. Some of you have never really trusted your entire life. You will find that, as you move closer to trust, you will be releasing control. Let control go. It is just a protective measure you have taught yourself to love. Now you are going to teach yourself to love trust.

❧

When you first began to shift consciousness you may have felt a great 'gust' of light sweep into your life. This is how you usually begin to awaken. Usually you will begin to see things differently, and gradually you will begin to change your perspective. The big gust of the light is what keeps you going. You remember how good it felt when you first began to discover your answers and you continue to search for that same good feeling.

As you search yourself and heal yourself, that light will begin to come to you once again in small doses. The light came in a gust at first because you opened a new part of you and allowed a shift to take place. Some of you have bigger shifts than others due to the fact that you are more pliable to change. As your shifts occur you begin to miss the light and feel only the darkness that is constantly being released from within. This will change once you reach the core of your pain, and you will be allowed to rest and feel like you are coming back from the pain or what you might call hell. As you return you will have left behind huge burdens and huge amounts of judgment. Some of you will even release old trapped pain from many past lives. It all depends on how deeply you can penetrate your own armor and how easily you can go within to unblock the many blocks and clear room for more light and understanding.

As you get to the bigger blocks you will find that you have based your life and your beliefs on some of them. These are the biggest blocks for you because your emotional security is based on your beliefs. Remove your old beliefs and there goes your emotional security. You will find that you will not readily give up such strong beliefs. This is the programming that is the basis of what you see as your personality. If you give up these beliefs who will you be?

You will find it most difficult to "let go and trust." This process of letting go and trusting is what will bring you the greatest freedom and the greatest love, or light, into your life. It is so hard for you to let go of beliefs and patterns that you believe to be good for you, that you may spend a very long time just trying to unblock you. You are dealing with some very strong parts of you. The good news is that there is a shift that is constantly taking place and you will catch it soon. If you do not catch the shift now, you will catch it when it comes around again. It is like a spiral, or a merry-go-round. You catch on and ride around and up. You need not worry that you will be left behind. No one is left behind. Some catch the spiral up sooner but it does not matter. Everyone arrives when they are meant to.

As you learn to "let go and trust" you will know what it is to trust in God and yourself. You will know what it is to place yourself into God's care and to feel safe. No matter what happens you will feel safe. You will have come through your blocks that say, "I must protect myself at all costs." You won't feel the need for protection. You will be like a fearless child who knows that life and death are the same cycle of energy. You will no longer "fear" losing your life and you will no longer create unnecessary pain for yourself. As a child of God you feel "fearless" instead of "fearful." You know that you cannot get hurt unless you crave pain and you know that you are craving love, so everything turns to love. It is in a craving of love and the satiation of pain that you return to the angelic realms of trust and complete faith that God is you.

You will find this process most enjoyable when you reach it. You will also find that you no longer crave the thrill of the ride as you once did. You will lean more towards the joy of being and less towards the thrill of doing. This is all part of a process that takes time. I know that most of you hate to wait for anything but you will find that for every step there is a purpose and each inch takes you closer to you. You and God are one and you and God make a "whole." Do not be afraid of time. You do not fall apart as you grow old. Your programming just takes over and eventually kills you. You are releasing all the painful programming so that you will live in joy, peace and love. No more distress over how to live or how to not live.

You will end struggle as you release and let go of your need to survive, and you will float into your own true essence which has little-to-nothing to do with holding-on to survive. You have so much to learn and so much to undo and let go of. You have only just begun to glimpse how truly miraculous life can be. Trust and faith are your biggest light bringers!

⁂

As you begin to feel parts of you emerge you may not like how you are feeling. These emotions have been suppressed for a very long time and now it is time for you to own them and allow them to balance. As you begin to show your true feelings you may try to shut them off again. It is a good idea to simply allow them to come forward and to move through them. They may be feelings of hurt, rejection, pride, hatred, revenge, jealousy, unsatisfied urges or any number of things that have been pushed down in you. Remember - when you begin to heal, all of your unhealed places will surface. Don't try to stuff them back down. Begin to move into them and, eventually, you will come through them and they will no longer be a block.

As you learn to grow into yourself you will also learn to sit and "observe" these parts without getting too caught up in the drama. If you can be the observer you are doing well. This does not mean shutting down or shutting off feelings. True observance is the ability to watch your own emotions rise and fall without acting out and getting into the emotional drama.

As you learn to watch more and more trapped emotions rise to the surface, you will be allowed to release more and more. Don't panic! You can live through these releases without getting all stuck in them. The more adept you become at knowing that it is just you clearing old buried stuff, the easier it will be for you to deal with these parts of you without struggle. Once you learn to allow more parts to surface you will be able to feel freer. These parts have bogged you down and weighted you down, and kept you un-flexible and unable to select the many possibilities presented to you. The rules must go so that you might establish a new way of living; a freer way of being. You will truly become a free spirit.

When you learn how to be your own best friend by accepting "all" of you, you will be in a position to become much more than you have ever been. You will be allowed to love unconditionally and without reservation just as God loves. You will be unrestricted and you will be unbound and uninhibited. You will return to the freedom of the Garden of Eden. No more evil, no more rules. You could run naked without shame. Your sins were nonexistent and your fears were nonexistent. How can you not feel shame when you have so many rules to live by and there are so many who judge one another on a daily basis? How can you not feel pain and remorse about who you are? It is time to break these rules and to come up out of shame. You do not sin! Not ever! How can you sin when you are the creator of everything? Let go of this need to be good and you will let go of your need for punishment. Do not be good. You already are God. Do not worry about sin. It does not exist. Learn to love you and accept you.

Now; I want to caution you to remember, not only do you not sin, your neighbor does not sin. Neither of you sins. There are no sins. They do not do bad to you. You may allow uncomfortable and even painful experiences but it is in conjunction with another, and you may break out of the cycle of abuse just as you will give up the cycle of karma. There is no karma! There are no rules to follow. Be free and do not be afraid to "be." You will find that freedom frightens you more than anything. You have lived in a prison for so long that you do not know how to leave it, even when the door is opened for you.

As you grow in strength you will begin to see your weaknesses. Your weaknesses could be anything from fear to anger to killing. You could simply fear life or fear power or fear anyone who is angry with you. You could also be the angry one and be draining your own energy in that way. Anger is dense and requires a great deal of energy. You may also be afraid of your own anger. If you are afraid of your own anger you may find that you are doubly drained by the simple fact that you are afraid of you. When you are afraid of power you begin to control so you will not lose to the power. You may begin to hold tightly to your control position and this too will weaken you.

You will find that as you clear and release all of your blocked energy you will be allowing energy to move. Some of this energy has sat in you for a very long time. Some of this energy has been growing like a huge festering wound. Some of this energy will not feel very good to you when you finally bring it to the surface. Eventually you will want to face the fact that you are everything that you feel. You are not just your thoughts you are also the feelings that file through you. You are your feelings and you are attached to your feelings by your need to feel. When you need to feel pain you will draw pain. It may even be false pain. You have a thing that you call sympathy pain and this is what most pain is. It is being out of touch with your own feelings to the extent that you still punish you for something that occurred lifetimes ago, or it may be something that occurred years ago. At any rate, you will find that your pain is confused and unnecessary. It is not real. It is brought up to make you feel bad. In some cases the pain is imagined by you to make you feel bad about yourself.

You may create your own imagined pain. I will give you an example: You come home from work and no one is there to greet you. You feel a little bad about that but basically it's no big deal. You look in the refrigerator for your leftover pizza that is your favorite flavor. You love leftover pizza, but your pizza is gone. Now you begin to get upset. Someone is taking your favorite food and no one was home to greet you. Now you go in to lie down in front of the television and watch your favorite show. The television is gone. Now you are afraid. Did someone come in and steal your television and your pizza? And where is your family? Did they just leave or are they in danger somewhere? Now you begin to panic. You call the neighbors, who do not answer, and so you call the police. The police tell you a pizza and stolen television are not that serious and your family has not been missing long enough to file a report.

Now you sit and wonder. Then you remember the fight you had last night with your spouse. "Oh my God!" you think, "She took the kids and left. The pizza was their favorite food and they couldn't survive without the television to watch cartoons." Now you begin to punish yourself for trusting your wife. You call yourself stupid and you swear that you will get your kids back, not to mention that new television. So now you sit down with your upset feelings and begin to plan how to best handle the situation. Your fight last night wasn't the worst you've ever had, but she was probably at her limit. Now you decide to change the locks on the door. You are upset and want your power back. You have been wronged! So you call someone to change the locks. He says he'll be right out. You wait until he gets the job done and then you go down the street to have a drink.

Twenty minutes later your wife tries to get in the house. She has the kids in tow because she could not find a sitter. She is carrying your new television that she just had repaired so you can watch the big game this weekend. She also has a pizza for you because her friend came over to fix the sink for free and so she offered him coffee and yesterday's pizza. Now she stands at the door and cannot get in. She is confused. The kids are yelling. She begins to worry. Why aren't you home? The kids are irritable. Where are you? She shouldn't have to take on all the jobs of repair and then not be able to get in her own home. Where are you?

You may find that a great deal of confusion and pain is created by the brain's need to stir things up. How does one's brain develop a need to stir things up? By being programmed long ago to bring on pain. It is programmed to hurt you in some way when you do not follow certain rules that were somehow programmed into your sensory banks. This is much too detailed to go into right now, but just understand that you all create positions and situations that are totally imagined. You must break out of your weakness for this type of drama. When you learn to trust, you will be breaking this programming. There is a big difference between "fear that something is going on" and the "intuitive message that something is amiss." Be careful in your judgments until you know how you are programmed to sabotage your own good. You all have this need in you to destroy. It will come to the surface in various ways. Try to learn by it and to observe rather than "act out" a drama.

By the way, the police were finally sent to the home by the neighbors who saw someone breaking in through a window. Then the wife was hauled off to jail for breaking and entering until, of course, she was able to prove it was her home. You see, her identification still had their old address on it so everything was quite a mess. You turned up later to explain how you had gotten upset and changed the locks. She's now very upset, and you are feeling stupid, and the kids are cranky and irritable. You may never speak again just to punish one another. This is how you use revenge. You all have your ways of getting even!

As you learn to evolve in this fashion it will become easier and easier for you to maintain light. Your main purpose is to become light and to know light. Light is the essence of your beingness so you might say that your main purpose is to know yourself.

Be true to yourself and learn to love yourself. You are the one and only you on this plane. You have many parts to the one and only you, but it is still yours. Own you. Do not push you away by blaming everyone else for your creations. Allow yourself to know who you are by allowing yourself to see how you trick and lie and cheat in order to stay in denial. Allow yourself to see through your lies every time you try to blame someone else for your existence. Allow yourself to see the truth and to know who you really are and how you change what you do in order to suit yourself and to keep yourself in camouflage. You will find that you are very deceitful and very tricky when it comes to acting out your stuff so that you will not catch on how you are the creator. You want to be one way so you simply *pretend* that you are until you begin to believe you are. Then you project that belief out and you show everyone who you are.

You are all grand actors and this is the time to take off your mask and stop pretending to yourself. You are coming out of a trance that has kept you in denial. When you come out you may not be in very good shape at first. You may be disoriented with your life and a little confused about who you are. This is change and this is waking up. You are beginning to wake up so that you might be conscious. Wouldn't it be nice to be conscious? If you were more conscious you would have trust in absolutely everything that occurs in your life. Everything would simply fall into place because you would not be criticizing nor punishing you or anyone else. Everyone would love everyone else because, with trust, there is no need to fight and argue. With trust everyone will *know* that everything is in divine order.

When you learn to trust, you will see your entire world change. You will see how things come to you more easily, as you are no longer blocking and pushing things and people away. You don't now, you say? Yes you do! You create it all. You created the blocks long ago that keep you in your self-righteousness and safe from all sin. Well, the problem is that now you are separated from everyone and everything, and you are feeling abandoned and lost. The only thing is that you do not even realize how you are the one who has abandoned everyone and everything in order to protect and stay safe. You will find that trust provides a much better way.

As you learn to recognize your patterns that separate you from others you will begin to feel a little uneasy at the idea of rejoining the others. You have lived with this idea of separation for so long now that it will take some time to get you to fully integrate with the rest. Once you have integrated with the others you will no longer feel abandoned, as you will have reunited not only the self, you will also have reunited your creation or outer world. It all begins within and then is reflected outward. So, if you wish to end loneliness and feelings of separation you may begin by healing the split in you. It started with the belief that you are bad or good. You are neither. You are simply God!

❧❧❧

As you learn to distinguish between addictive old habits and your intuitive ability you will find that you are learning how to be your own best friend and guide. Most of you have set up patterns that will feel impossible to break. This is due, in part, to the fact that your patterns are so well used. Do you often wonder at the stupidity of others? This is most likely your pattern. You see everyone around you as stupid in order to feel safe and on-top like the smart one. You set this game up long ago, maybe because you were treated as the stupid one or maybe you were called stupid. Now you have the need to point out the mistakes in others or just to notice how dumb they can and, often do, act. When you look for stupidity you will find it. This is due to your ability to make things what you want them to be regardless of what they really are. As you learn to detect your own patterns you will be allowed to change them. Once you have changed them you will begin to see all of "your world" differently. You will also begin to like your world a whole lot better.

Now; if you have been programmed to be superior to others, you will find it difficult to accept others and to find compatibility. You will believe that you are smarter and more achieved in certain areas of your life. You will claim that no one understands you, when the reality is that you are creating a void to separate yourself from others. This void is created out of your need to find fault with others and your fault-finding is created by your need to feel safe. If you do not have a need to feel safe you will never criticize another. It is never necessary to criticize another. You do it out of insecurity. You will find that once you learn to love and accept you, you will no longer criticize you, nor will you criticize the boss, nor the laws, nor the condition of your world. You will learn to love and accept, because you have learned to love and accept you.

As you begin to uncover the parts of you that have been criticizing and tearing down you, you will feel very put upon. You will be uncovering this part of you that just refuses to give you or anyone else a break. This part of you is very strong in you and it may not feel too good to release it. It will put you down for everything that you do and it will criticize you no matter what. This may be a very difficult time for you. You will be releasing your need to be controlled by your inner voice. This will in turn release your need to control others.

As you let go of such a big part of you I want you to know that you will have accomplished a very great achievement. To let go of the critic in you is to let go of your need to control everything. God will finally have the opportunity to live in your life without being criticized for being God. You see, your critic self even decides if God is stupid or not. Your critic self is set up to enforce the rules and when God comes along and says, "Stop following the rules," your critic will judge this God as crazy and enforce the rules even stronger. You must learn to see your game. You are programmed like a computer and you are creating everything by judging it and saying what it is. Do not allow yourself to be the smart one. Playing it safe by hiding one's insecurities is how you set yourself up for this type of separation. You feel that you cannot trust, so you shut yourself off from others by convincing yourself that you are different or that your situation is different. You are not. You are all the same.

When you learn to break down your own patterns you will find out why you do what you do. This will allow you to see how you treat others, which is directly related to how you treat yourself. You are the one you are always seeing in everyone else. You are the one you call stupid when you call them stupid. If you have a problem with someone else it is only a direct reflection of your problem with you!

&⁓

When you learn how to overcome your own programming you will be in a position of power. You have never before "let go" in such a big way. As you "let go" of more and more of you, you will gain more of you. The part you are letting go of is a defensive mechanism that takes a great deal of energy. For some of you it has become a full-time job just to protect your way of viewing things. If you are very defensive in your conversations and if you think you are right, you are more than likely putting your defenses up. If you find it necessary to call everyone on their mistakes or to correct them, you are in your defensiveness. If you argue, you are defending. If you struggle for dominance, you are defensive to the extent that you are fighting and becoming offensive.

"Let it go." Let everything go. Do not be afraid to lose this type of power. It is not really power, it is weakness. When you struggle to maintain your dignity it is only because you feel like you have no dignity. This is due to low self-esteem. Do not fight others to prove how good you are. Allow yourself to be loved enough to "know" how good you are. If you already know that you are good, it might not affect you if someone infers that you are not. If you walk down the street and someone says to you, "You're a bum," but you know you have a million dollars in the bank, does what that one person says affect you? Not at all. You know it's not true. Your only problem right now is that you believe you are a bum, or a bad person. So if anyone treats you poorly or insinuates you're not good enough, you freak out. This is due to low self-esteem. You do not straighten out the one who sent the message to show you who you are, you straighten out you. Let go of self-loathing and self-hatred by changing your programming.

So far, it has been very difficult to change the biggest part of you. This part is fear. As we have gone along in this series of books we have gained a great deal of insight into the inner workings of the self. There is a great deal yet to discuss and you will find it all interesting and enlightening. The reason this information is so repetitive is to give you the opportunity to absorb the information. If you are told a million different times that you are bad, you will begin to believe that you are bad. In the same way, if you are told a million different times that you are good; you will begin to believe that you are already good. This too is how I will convince you that you are God, the creator. You are now in a position to make great change and great shifts within the self, especially if you have read along in the order that this information has been given.

You see, there is a reason for the vagueness in certain areas of this information. There is also a reason for the abruptness and the boldness of certain statements. Everything in this series of books is meant to trigger one's inner domain. You will find many who are not yet ready to be triggered in such a manner. For those of you who are still with us, I wish to thank you for your undying attention. You will be happy to know that we will write our next book soon. Liane is doing well and has released a great deal of pain, both from past life and from this life. She is still agreeable to doing my work and I intend to write a few more books through her body as long as she consents. You will be happy to know that our next book is titled *We All Walk Together*. This is a good title as it shows how we all are in this soup together.

As you go along your path try to remember "you are not alone." No matter how out of focus and out of sync you feel, you are part of everyone and everything else. The separation is illusion. It is created by the need to feel safe in aloneness. Now the aloneness only feels empty and painful. You are returning now to the flock and you will feel like you belong and you will feel love. Your own love will "open up" your entire world and you will "feel" it differently. Until next time I bid you a fond "I love you."

God's Pen

I first heard the voice of God in 1988. I was sitting in my back yard reading a book when this big booming voice interrupted with, "I am God and I will not come to you by any other name." I felt like the voice was everywhere - inside of me as well as in the sky around me. I was so frightened that I ran in my bedroom to hide.

This was not the first time that I heard voices. I had been communicating with my own spirit guide or soul for about a year. I guess my depth of fear regarding God, and all that he represented to me at the time, was just too much.

I spent two days trying to avoid the voice of God, which was patiently waiting for me to respond. By the second day I was exhausted from lack of sleep and decided to give in and talk with him. This turned out to be the greatest gift and best decision of my life.

The first book, *God Spoke through Me to Tell You to Speak to Him*, shows my evolution from communicating with my soul to communicating with the Big Guy. It took a couple years for me to be comfortable communicating with God. My fear of a punishing God was big! That has most definitely changed and I now think of God as my partner and best friend.

In the beginning the voice of God would wake me in the middle of the night and tell me it was time to write. He said I had promised to do this work (I assumed he was talking about the soul/spirit me). I would drag myself up to a sitting position and watch in amazement as my hand flew across the page, while I tried to keep up by reading what was being written.

It was always so much fun to wake up the next morning and grab my notebook to see what God had written during the night. After some time the voice stopped waking me and I became comfortable picking up my pen and writing for God first thing in the morning. I think in the beginning I had to be awakened while still semi-conscious from sleep so I wouldn't object too much to the information that was being channeled through me.

As I grew less and less afraid (and more trusting) of God, he was able to communicate greater information. Some of the information is quit controversial, but I felt it important to just let it be and not censor it. I present the writings here to you as they were given to me. I have edited a little (mostly the more personal information regarding myself) and I have used a pen name for privacy reasons. I asked God for a good pen name and he guided me to Liane which (I was told) in Hebrew means "God has answered."

At one point I became a little concerned about my sanity in all this, so I went to a hypnotherapist to find out what I was doing. Under hypnosis I saw this incredibly huge beam of light with a voice coming from within it. It was a giant "loving light" and felt so comforting and kind. It felt like that's where I came from. After that I stopped worrying about my sanity. If this is crazy, I think it's a very good kind of crazy to be....

In loving light, Liane

Loving Light Books

Available at:
Loving Light Books - www.lovinglightbooks.com
Amazon - www.amazon.com
Barnes & Noble - www.barnesandnoble.com